CAMPAIGN • 248

CORONEL AND FALKLANDS 1914

Duel in the South Atlantic

MICHAEL McNALLY   ILLUSTRATED BY PETER DENNIS

Series editor Marcus Cowper

First published in Great Britain in 2012 by Osprey Publishing,
Midland House, West Way, Botley, Oxford OX2 0PH, UK
43-01 21st Street, Suite 220B, Long Island City, NY 11101, USA
Email: info@ospreypublishing.com

Osprey Publishing is part of the Osprey Group.

A CIP catalogue record for this book is available from the British Library.

ISBN: 978 1 84908 674 5
PDF e-book ISBN: 978 1 84908 675 2
E-pub e-book ISBN: 978 1 78200 298 7

Editorial by Ilios Publishing Ltd, Oxford, UK (www.iliospublishing.com)
Page layout by The Black Spot
Index by Judy Oliver
Typeset in Myriad Pro and Sabon
Maps by Bounford.com
3D bird's-eye view by The Black Spot
Battlescene illustrations by Peter Dennis
Originated by PDQ Media, Bungay, UK
Printed in China through World Print Ltd.

13 14 15 16 17   11 10 9 8 7 6 5 4 3

www.ospreypublishing.com

ARTIST'S NOTE

Readers may care to note that the original paintings from which the color
plates in this book were prepared are available for private sale. The
Publishers retain all reproduction copyright whatsoever. All enquiries
should be addressed to:

Peter Dennis,
Fieldhead,
The Park,
Mansgfield,
Notts,
NG18 2AT, UK

Email: magieh@ntl.com

The Publishers regret that they can enter into no correspondence upon
this matter.

DEDICATION

As always, I'd like to thank my wife and family (Petra, Stephen, Elena-Rose
and Liam) for their patience over the last year or so during the research and
writing of this book, and of course to everyone who has cast a critical eye
over the manuscript as it took shape. I'd also like to offer special thanks to
my editor – Marcus Cowper – for his words of encouragement when things
were going right and, just as importantly, when they were going wrong.
And so, this one's for you Marcus!

THE WOODLAND TRUST

Osprey Publishing are supporting the Woodland Trust, the UK's leading
woodland conservation charity, by funding the dedication of trees.

CONTENTS

THE STRATEGIC SITUATION

OPPOSITE: The end of the Nürnberg following the battle of the Falkland Islands in a print after Stöwer. (Author's collection)

BELOW: SMS *Scharnhorst im Fernosten*. In more peaceable times, this print – after Stöwer – shows *Scharnhorst* in her tropical colour scheme. (Author's collection)

At midnight on Tuesday, 4 August 1914, the world changed for ever when Great Britain issued an ultimatum to both Germany and France. It required that, in the event of hostilities between them, both countries would respect the neutrality of Belgium, enshrined within the 1839 Treaty of London. Britain, as one of the treaty's signatories, was obliged to defend this condition; France, aware that she needed time to organize her armed forces for her own defence, immediately acceded to British demands; Germany, on the other hand, merely replied that whilst she would not annex any Belgian territory – thereby tacitly respecting the kingdom's sovereignty – she could not allow France the opportunity to use this same terrain to launch a pre-emptive attack. Berlin was again pressed to accede to British demands. No response was received and Whitehall sent instructions to the fleet to commence hostilities.

Heer und Flotte 1914.

Serie Nr. 888. Bild 3. Großer Kreuzer „Scharnhorst".

Willy Stöwer

HMS *Triumph*. Like *Canopus* this outdated battleship was hurriedly pressed into service in order to meet Maximilian von Spee's threat and manned by a mixture of reservists and Army personnel. (IWM, Q040369)

Britain had been lucky to have at her disposal the services of perhaps the greatest of her reforming admirals, Admiral Sir John 'Jacky' Fisher. He had not only embraced modern technology and the development of bigger and better warships but was also – in the face of Germany's provocative Naval Construction Programme – not afraid to 'wield the administrative axe' where necessary and his draconian measures resulted in savings that went a long way towards the Royal Navy redefining itself as a more modern force during the pre-war years. Indeed Britain took the lead in ship construction with the commissioning in 1906 of HMS *Dreadnought*, the world's first 'all heavy gun' warship and the epitome of Fisher's dictum that firepower and speed would be the two deciding factors in future naval combat. This revolutionary design would, for two decades, become the yardstick by which all fleets were measured, and the acquisition of such vessels become a sign of prestige that would help to drive at least one nation into near bankruptcy and another into World War I, on the side of the Central Powers.

Unlike its counterpart and despite its name, the German Imperial Navy did not come into being because of the needs or requirements of empire, but simply from Kaiser Wilhelm II's desire to beard his English relatives by striking out at British naval tradition. In his own mind, he wanted to meet his uncle, King Edward VII (and then his cousin, King George V) on equal terms. But it was one thing to fantasize about having a large fleet, and another to make it a reality and when, after a naval dinner at Kiel, he asked where the future of the German Navy lay, one of the guests, replied with one word – 'battleships'. This simple response lay perfectly in keeping with the Kaiser's own inclinations and would propel the officer – Alfred von Tirpitz – into a career which would see him dominate the German Navy for over 20 years.

Ostensibly, the aim behind the German programme, known collectively as the *'Novelles'* or 'Navy Laws', was to prevent a repetition of 1870 when the French fleet was able to bombard the German coastline at will. Now, with the Dual Entente between France and Russia, it was conceivable that Germany could be dragged into a war on two fronts with the best way to adequately protect her coastline would be to have a large enough fleet to be able to take the maritime offensive.

After the turn of the century, following the successful passing of the Second Navy Bill, the grateful emperor had ennobled his bourgeois protégé and the newly created Admiral von Tirpitz began to pursue an objective that, for the time being at least, he was wise enough to conceal from both foreign and domestic observers – the creation of a modern fleet. This fleet, whilst unable to challenge Britain on a global basis, would in a single, specific theatre of operations be strong enough to render uncertain the outcome of any major engagement so that, even in victory, Britain would suffer such damage at German hands as to endanger her position as the world's premier naval power.

With Britain's senior naval command changing with each change of government, the continual favour that von Tirpitz enjoyed at both the Reichstag and the Imperial Court ensured that the German Navy displayed consistency at the highest levels, thus ensuring a similar consistency in naval construction that was to prove decisive during the coming conflict. Whilst Fisher was obliged to weed out obsolete vessels before he could press ahead with his overhaul of the Royal Navy, his German counterpart was simply able to divert Imperial funds into his new construction programme; Fisher's vision was of fast warships which would overwhelm the enemy with a combination of speed and firepower, von Tirpitz's, however, was one where the vessels could absorb significant enemy damage and still be able to fight their guns.

'The greatest protection' – British 12in. guns in action. (IWM, Q053498)

TOP
Both sides pressed civilian vessels into service as military auxiliaries – *Empress of Asia* was one of the many scouts employed during the search for *Emden*. (IWM, Q058071)

BOTTOM
HMS *Glasgow*. Unable to influence the outcome of Coronel, *Glasgow* played a creditable role at the Falklands and in finally bringing *Dresden* to bay. (IWM, Q021286)

This 'risk strategy', as it has become known, was clearly based upon the premise that the Imperial Navy would only need to achieve local equality in order to avoid a naval catastrophe, as her potential 'enemy' would be wary of achieving a major victory at the cost of losing its own naval primacy. On paper this argument seemed watertight, but it fatally ignored the fact that Britain had no need to risk a fleet engagement and instead could rely on numbers and her unique geographical position simply to blockade the German coast. In all likelihood it would therefore be Germany herself who would instigate any naval confrontation, and behind much of von Tirpitz's planning lay a single overriding concern, the fear of which would drive him to push ever grander proposals through the Reichstag. In August 1807, Britain had attacked the then neutral Denmark and, under cover of an armed landing, seized the Danish fleet in Copenhagen harbour in order to 'prevent' it from falling into French hands. It was this spectre of his ships being

'Copenhagened' as such an operation had subsequently become known, that haunted Tirpitz during what was referred to as 'the time of greatest danger' i.e. the time before a sufficient proportion of the fleet had been completed.

The Kaiserliche Marine, with few exceptions, would ultimately concentrate its entire strength in home waters, so that at the beginning of World War I it had few overseas deployments. In the Caribbean, for example, the Imperial Flag was flown by the light cruiser *Dresden* (shortly to be replaced by *Karlsruhe*), whilst East African waters were patrolled by *Königsberg*. The jewel in the crown, however, operated from the naval base at Tsingtao in China and was organized around the modern armoured cruisers *Scharnhorst* and *Gneisenau*, supported by the lesser-armed but just as modern *Leipzig*, *Nürnberg* and *Emden*. They were officially referred to as 'die Ostasiengeschwader' (East Asia Squadron) and simply known to their crews and the German people, as 'die Geschwader' (the Squadron).

Accordingly, Berlin became overconfident and was complacent in the belief that Britain would remain peaceful in the afterglow of her 'century of splendid isolation'. But stung into carrying out its own naval construction programme, the Royal Navy would, in fact, not only remain ahead of the Kaiserliche Marine in the race to build bigger and better capital ships, but also had in Fisher a leader who, deciding upon a course of action, would terrier-like pursue it to its final conclusion.

Presciently, Fisher was convinced that a major, global conflict or 'Armageddon', as he termed it, would ensue in October 1914. In preparation for this he intended that the Royal Navy would be prepared for any

Unable to answer the superior enemy gunnery adequately, the fate of the woefully under-armed *Monmouth* was sealed in the opening moments of Coronel. (IWM, Q039657)

challenges it might face, maintaining that its modernization was being held back by the costs of manning and maintaining a large number of ships that he viewed as obsolete. Fisher would remain unperturbed in the face of a massive public backlash at the planned restructure and, on his orders, more than 150 vessels of various classes were either sold off or placed into the Naval Reserve. The saving, in both cost and manpower, generated by this austerity constituted the first steps in the enforced modernization of the navy; despite the implementation of an accelerated naval construction programme, which formed the British response to Germany's Navy Acts, the Royal Navy's planned expenditure for 1905 would be almost 10 per cent lower than for the period prior to his appointment.

Fisher was convinced of the need for improvement in all areas of naval gunnery and brought this belief with him when he assumed the chairmanship of the Committee on Design. Almost immediately work began on the development of one of the most radical designs in naval history: a fast, 'all big gun' battleship, whose turreted armament would be deployed specifically to maximize its firepower in all directions. Coupled with an increase in protective armour plating, and capable of relatively high speeds, this new battleship would be far superior to all vessels of all nations then in service. It was from this superiority that the class of vessel would derive its name – *Dreadnought*.

Eventually, Fisher began to think laterally, and plans were soon laid to marry his gunnery theories to the next-smallest class of vessels in the Royal Navy – the cruisers. The workhorses of a modern navy, these vessels had evolved to become adept at several tasks, ranging from scouting in advance of the main battle fleets to independent action and warfare against the enemy's merchant navy. They ranged from fast light cruisers, which relied on their speed to perform their duties, to heavier vessels, which would act as principal warships in foreign waters, often as squadron flagships. Before Fisher's promotion in 1904, most nations, Britain included, had sought to enhance the

Sturdee's flagship, *Invincible*, narrowly escaped destruction during the closing stages of the Falklands, a fate that would overtake her at Jutland two years later. (IWM, Q039274)

capability of these latter ships by the simple expedient of additional armour plating, thereby gaining them the distinction of being 'armoured' or 'protected' cruisers. Fisher's plan, however, was more radical. His proposal was simply to build larger cruisers which would still be capable of reaching high speeds but which, at the cost of less armour protection, would carry heavy guns, similar to those on his beloved dreadnoughts, relying on speed to catch the enemy and firepower to destroy him.

Informally referred to as 'Fisher's greyhounds', this new class of warship – the battle cruiser – was theoretically suited to both fleet and independent action. It represented the latest embodiment of the eternal debate over which aspect of ship design was of paramount importance: speed and manoeuvrability, protection or firepower. Fatally, Fisher and the British designers got it wrong. Although the statistics of *Invincible*, the first ship of this type and later to be Sturdee's flagship at the Falklands, were indeed impressive, the design was fatally flawed as the ship was woefully underprotected.

Britain's outspoken admiral did not voice his opinions on just domestic matters and, whilst preparing his charge for the ultimate test, he cast about for the identity of the most likely future foe, stating that: 'the new German Navy has come into existence; it is a navy of the most efficient type and is so fortunately constituted that it is able to constitute almost all of its fleet including almost all of its battleships at its home ports.' It would be true to say that had Fisher been able to scrap the entire Royal Navy and rebuild it from the bottom upwards, it would most likely have resembled the very force that he was planning to engage and destroy. However, in times of war Britain had to be strong in several theatres, whilst Germany had merely to display her strength in home waters.

THE PACIFIC THEATRE

Upon the outbreak of hostilities, and despite the fact that the area covered almost 92,000,000 square miles of open water, the Admiralty in London remained firm in its belief that the naval forces deployed in and around the Pacific and Indian Oceans were more than sufficient to meet its requirements in times of both peace and war.

To accomplish the task Great Britain deployed several naval task forces in the region: the China Station under the command of Vice Admiral Sir Thomas H. M. Jerram, whose principal forces consisted of one pre-dreadnought battleship, two armoured and two light cruisers; the East Indies Station under Rear Admiral Sir Richard Peirse (one pre-dreadnought and two light cruisers) and the Cape of Good Hope Station under Rear Admiral Sir Reginald King-Hall (three light cruisers) to which were added the Dominion Naval Forces of Australia and New Zealand which had been placed under Admiralty authority and were commanded by Rear Admiral Sir George Patey (one battle cruiser, seven light cruisers). In addition to her own forces, Britain also received overall direction of a number of allied vessels, namely, the French armoured cruiser *Montcalm* and light cruiser *Dupleix* and the Russian armoured cruisers *Askold* and *Zhemchug*.

On paper at least, the total strength of this combined force would ensure a relatively quick and easy victory over the ships of von Spee's Ostasiengeschwader. However the potential area of operations was huge and any superiority was fatally weakened by Britain's own war plans which dictated that admirals were

Vice Admiral Sir Thomas H. M. Jerram, Commander of the RN China Station tasked with neutralizing the Ostasiengeschwader on the outbreak of hostilities. (IWM, 003141)

to give absolute priority to the provision of armed escorts for troop convoys originating in or sailing through their areas of responsibility. Therefore, in the early months of the war, a significant amount of time was wasted in escorting an Anglo-Indian Expeditionary Force to the coast of German East Africa, and the Australia and New Zealand Army Corps (ANZAC) to Europe. In addition escorts had to be provided for the movement of two smaller expeditions – Australian troops to annex the German colony of New Guinea, and New Zealand forces to occupy Samoa. This resulted in Britain's naval forces being fatally dispersed at a crucial period whilst the German admiral made his initial moves.

Sitting on the sidelines was the Japanese fleet whose commitment, if made, would signal the death knell of von Spee's squadron. Although the Anglo-Japanese Treaty of 1902 (renewed in 1911) covered the mutual protection of each other's merchant navy in times of war, it precluded the enforced involvement of either signatory in a war against a European state. It looked, therefore, as if the largest naval power in the region would remain firmly neutral upon the outbreak of hostilities, but British diplomats correctly reasoned that Japan would respond favourably to any British requests for assistance.

VON SPEE SAILS

As events in Europe unfolded, the Marine Kabinett in Berlin issued the following directive:

> In the event of a war against Great Britain, ships abroad are to carry out 'cruiser warfare' unless otherwise ordered. Those vessels which are not fit to carry out cruiser warfare are to fit out as auxiliary cruisers. The areas of operations are the Atlantic, the Pacific and the Indian Oceans.... The aim of cruiser warfare is to damage enemy trade; this is to be effected by engaging equal or inferior enemy forces.... The conduct of the naval war in home waters is to be assisted by holding down as many of the enemy's forces as possible in foreign waters.

By way of clarification, the section specific to the Pacific Ocean continued:

> The chief aim of all operations is to damage British trade. Operations, apart from the relative strength of the belligerent forces, will depend mainly on the possibility of securing regular coal supplies. This will also determine the selection of the area of operations: the prompt departure of a ship to this area will oblige the enemy to search for her and consequently to dilute her forces, thus affording opportunities to achieve tactical success against isolated elements of the enemy fleet. By attacking the main trade routes, we may succeed in suspending British traffic to the Far East for some time. The best means of affording relief to Tsingtao is for the ships of the Cruiser Squadron to retain their freedom of movement for as long as is possible. If, on the outbreak of war, circumstances for the Cruiser Squadron are especially favourable, it may be in a position immediately to strike the enemy forces a decisive blow and cripple the enemy's trade and maritime supremacy in the Far East.

Instead of issuing the confusing and often contradictory orders that would characterize instructions from the Admiralty in London, the German High

The Pacific region showing naval concentrations and von Spee's voyage

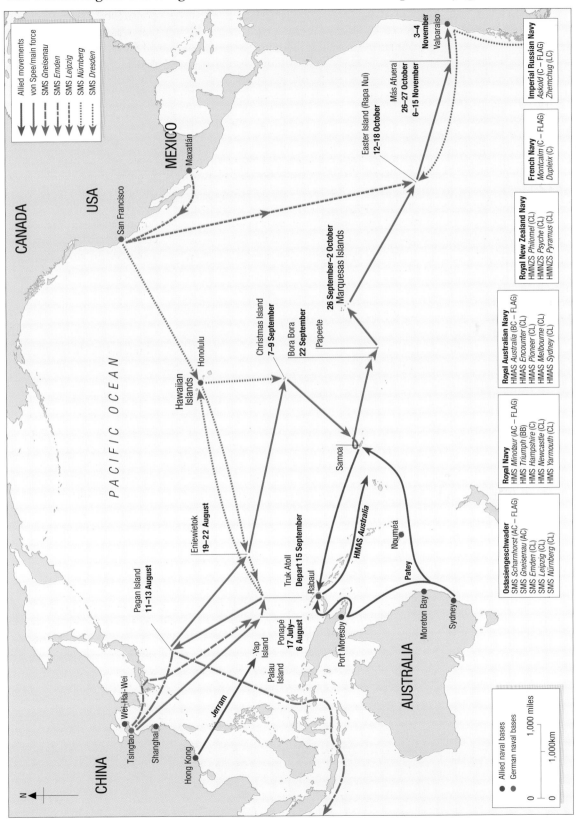

Legend:

Allied movements
von Spee/main force
SMS *Gneisenau*
SMS *Emden*
SMS *Leipzig*
SMS *Nürnberg*
SMS *Dresden*

● Allied naval bases
● German naval bases

0   1,000 miles
0   1,000km

N

Ostasiengeschwader
SMS *Scharnhorst* (AC – FLAG)
SMS *Gneisenau* (AC)
SMS *Emden* (CL)
SMS *Leipzig* (CL)
SMS *Nürnberg* (CL)

Royal Navy
HMS *Minotaur* (AC – FLAG)
HMS *Triumph* (BB)
HMS *Hampshire* (C)
HMS *Newcastle* (CL)
HMS *Yarmouth* (CL)

Royal Australian Navy
HMAS *Australia* (BC – FLAG)
HMAS *Encounter* (CL)
HMAS *Pioneer* (C)
HMAS *Melbourne* (CL)
HMAS *Sydney* (CL)

Royal New Zealand Navy
HMNZS *Philomel* (CL)
HMNZS *Psyche* (CL)
HMNZS *Pyramus* (CL)

French Navy
Montcalm (C – FLAG)
Dupleix (C)

Imperial Russian Navy
Askold (C – FLAG)
Zhemchug (LC)

Place labels:

CANADA
USA
MEXICO
Maxatlán
San Francisco

CHINA
Tsingtao
Wei-Hai-Wei
Shanghai
Hong Kong

PACIFIC OCEAN

Honolulu
Hawaiian Islands
Eniewietok **19–22 August**

Pagan Island **11–13 August**
Yap Island
Palau Island
Ponapé **17 July– 6 August**
Truk Atoll **Depart 15 September**
Rabaul
Jerram
Port Moresby
Moreton Bay
Sydney
AUSTRALIA
Nouméa
Patey
Samoa
HMAS *Australia*

Christmas Island **7–9 September**
Bora Bora **22 September**
Papeete
Marquesas Islands **26 September–2 October**
Easter Island (Rapa Nui) **12–18 October**
Mas Afuera **26–27 October 6–15 November**
Valparaiso **3–4 November**

13

Back-breaking work. Here the crew of HMAS *Australia* loads coal by hand. (IWM, Q18754)

Command had immediately hit upon the nub of the problem that would face the commanders of their overseas assets – access to a regular fuel supply. Although, in peacetime, ships could coal and resupply as desired, in wartime they could refuel in a neutral country only once every three months, preferring to coal – however intermittently – from friendly or, in the event of their capture, enemy ships.

Berlin, however, was half a world away and, despite these warnings, colonial life went on as usual, with Admiral Jerram – aboard HMS *Minotaur* – making a courtesy visit in June to the German base at Tsingtao. Shortly after Jerram's departure, von Spee made the final preparations for a summer voyage that would take the squadron across the Marianas, Carolines and Marshalls to German Samoa and then to New Guinea via the Bismarck Archipelago and from there back to Tsingtao on 20 September. Many of the officers had been stationed at Tsingtao for two years and on their return intended to take leave of the squadron and return to Germany via the Trans-Siberian Railway.

Gneisenau left port on 20 June and, after coaling at Nagasaki, continued on her voyage through the island chains, eventually reaching the Truk Atoll in the Carolines on 6 July, where she fell in with *Scharnhorst* which had reached the rendezvous first. The first indications of pending hostilities were received the following day when a message was received from Berlin in which von Spee was advised that 'the political situation is not entirely satisfactory'. As a result, the admiral decided to continue to Ponape – some 400 miles farther eastwards. Before he left Truk, he sent a message to Tsingtao giving orders that the light cruiser *Emden* was to act as escort to the squadron's auxiliaries which were to bring much-needed supplies to Ponape. On 27 July, another signal was received, this time advising, 'Strained relations between Dual Alliance and Triple Entente… Samoan cruise will most likely have to be abandoned… *Nürnberg* has been ordered to Tsingtao, everything else is left to your discretion.'

Aware that, after the East Asia Squadron itself, the most likely enemy target would be the base at Tsingtao, von Spee immediately countermanded *Nürnberg*'s movement orders. He also ordered *Leipzig* to San Francisco to purchase coal and gave orders to Karl von Müller, captain of the *Emden*, to complete his loading. *Nürnberg* was to meet the flagship at Ponape, whilst the other two were to sail to Pagan Island in the Marianas at their best possible speed. Elsewhere *Dresden*, the lone cruiser in the Caribbean, was told to sail for the Pacific and await further orders whilst en route.

On 1 August, Berlin transmitted the *Kriegsgefahr*, a message that meant that a state of war was imminent and that German commanders should take all necessary precautions. All ships at Ponape were stripped for battle and all personal and non-essential possessions were sent ashore – from now on they were on a war footing. The following day saw the announcement that Austria and Germany were now at war with France and Russia and on 5 August came the news that many officers found hard to believe, that Britain had elected to intervene on the side of her partners in the Triple Entente.

The following day, *Nürnberg* arrived at Ponape and the crews of all three vessels combined to coal the light cruiser. Then at 1700hrs, they once again put out to sea, the squadron retracing its steps to the rendezvous at Pagan, some thousand miles to the north. They arrived there at dawn on 11 August, several hours before *Emden* anxiously ushered her charges into the anchorage. As his squadron reassembled, von Spee considered his next move. His main problem

HMS *Minotaur* and SMS *Scharnhorst* at Tsingtao, Summer 1914. (IWM, HU64344)

Nürnberg, a Karlsruhe-class light cruiser and workhorse of the East Asia Squadron. (IWM, Q080704)

was that his most effective assets – *Scharnhorst* and *Gneisenau* – had originally been designed for service with the battle fleet, and were thus unsuited to the role that the Admiralty in Berlin seemed to have earmarked for them; in cruiser warfare speed is the decisive factor, the ability to choose to fight or to fly from a superior enemy, and not armour or armament.

Although von Spee had been given absolute discretion in his planning, geography was also to play a large part in his final decision; the most lucrative targets – the Australian ports – were all heavily defended and, lurking somewhere over the horizon, lay HMAS *Australia*, a modern battle cruiser that mounted eight 12in. guns. Because of this and the likelihood of Japanese

This Stöwer print shows the conflagration at Madras as *Emden*, unchallenged, bombards the port refineries, destroying millions of gallons of fuel. (Author's collection)

The voyage of the *Emden*

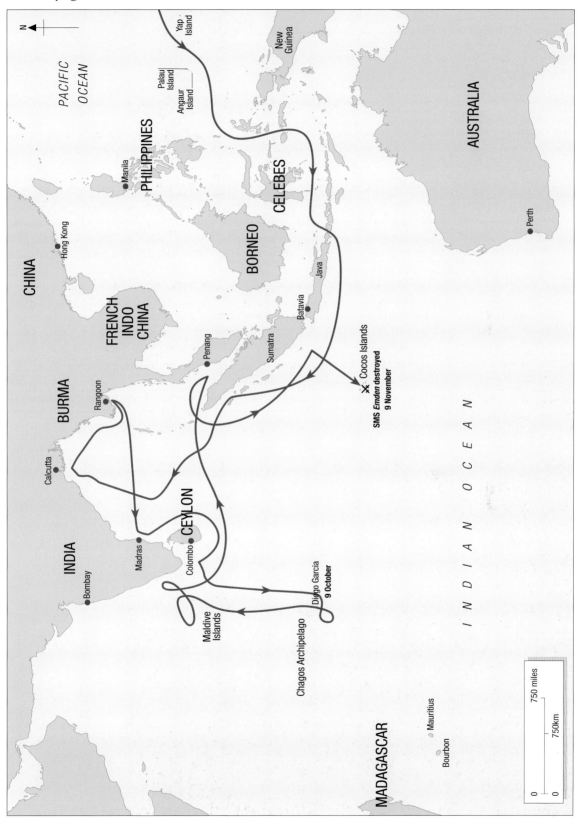

Admired by friend and foe alike, von Müller lived up to his promise by tying up significant enemy forces and diverting them from the search for von Spee. (Author's collection)

intervention, a return to Tsingtao was now out of the question. On the other hand a voyage westwards towards German East Africa would simply bring von Spee closer to growing numbers of British warships. He had only one real choice, to make for the eastern seaboard of the Americas where not only were there no known warships to prevent his interception of enemy trade, but also a number of neutral countries where he would have ample chances to resupply. In time he would be in close enough proximity to Cape Horn and the tip of South America and from there he could break into the South Atlantic waters and disappear in the vast expanse of the ocean before once again re-emerging to wreak havoc upon the enemy.

THE *EMDEN* AT LARGE

On the afternoon of 13 August, von Spee's 53rd birthday, he called a meeting aboard the *Scharnhorst* during which he explained to his captains his intention of sailing towards South America. One of the captains, von Müller of the *Emden*, ventured to disagree with his commander, stating that one ship sent in the opposite direction and aggressively commanded would not only cause great havoc amongst enemy merchant vessels but would also serve to confuse the enemy about the squadron's whereabouts and intentions. Von Spee considered the merits of von Müller's argument and he gave permission for the *Emden* and one of the colliers to leave the squadron and engage enemy merchantmen in the Indian Ocean. The same evening, the squadron left Pagan for the Marshall Islands.

Arriving in Indian waters, von Müller would soon repay this confidence, and between 10 and 14 September he sank eight steamers off the coast of Calcutta. *Emden* proceeded to Madras where, closing to 3,000 yards, von Müller bombarded the facility of the Burmah Oil Company. A month later, and disguised as a British warship, *Emden* sailed into Penang and torpedoed

Escorting a troop convoy to the Red Sea, *Sydney* was detached to investigate the presence of *Emden* at the Cocos Islands. (IWM, Q040261)

A gallant adversary. The wreck of the *Emden* run aground after the battle with *Sydney*. (IWM, Q02273)

the anchored Russian cruiser *Zhemchug* at point-blank range before leaving the harbour and sinking the French destroyer *Mousquet* as she valiantly tried to bar the German cruiser's escape. *Emden* was becoming perhaps the most hunted vessel on the high seas.

The end for the gallant raider came on 9 November when she approached the Cocos Islands with the intention of sending a party ashore. The light cruiser, HMAS *Sydney*, 55 miles to the north, was detached to deal with the enemy vessel. Von Müller was forced into battle with a more powerful opponent and was eventually driven upon a reef where she finally struck her colours.

ESCAPING THE TRAP

Upon reaching Eniwetok in the Marshalls on 19 August, von Spee was greeted with the bad news that the British had destroyed the wireless station at Yap in the Carolines. Without direct means of communication, he ordered *Nürnberg* back to Honolulu to advise Berlin of his intention to sail for Chile. On 7 September, having been joined by the armed merchantman *Cormoran* and four cargo vessels that had managed to escape Tsingtao before its investment by the Japanese, the squadron reached Christmas Island, where it was rejoined by *Nürnberg*.

Having received confirmation of the enemy's capture of Samoa, von Spee now decided upon a rapid descent upon the islands in anticipation of catching a number of allied vessels at anchor off the capital, Apia. If his luck held and one of these was *Australia*, he planned to engage her with torpedoes. Arriving on 14 September, he found the harbour deserted and ordered his ships to turn about and continue for Chile. However, when his radio operators intercepted a signal from Apia broadcasting his numbers and position he changed course, sailing north-west until he was out of sight of land before heading eastwards once more.

The next landfall was the French island of Bora Bora where, in a case of mistaken identity, the local authorities offered all possible assistance to 'the British admiral'. As the ships spent the day resupplying, a number of local dignitaries were gently interrogated by a succession of ship's officers who, maintaining the pretence by speaking only French or English, were especially

HMAS *Australia*. Perhaps the only vessel that could have engaged the Ostasiengeschwader during the initial stages of von Spee's voyage, the Australian battle cruiser was relegated to supporting the occupation of German colonies. (IWM, Q001795)

interested in the defences of Papeete, the capital of Tahiti. At the end of the day, as the German ships raised anchor, a huge tricolour was raised above the port by way of farewell salute and in response the Imperial Battle Ensign broke out from the mastheads of the Ostasiengeschwader. Realizing that they had been duped by the enterprising German admiral, the French authorities quickly sent a warning signal to Papeete, which was thus in a state of defence when von Spee's squadron hove into sight. Thwarted in his attempt to secure the port, von Spee continued eastwards, passing the Marquesas where he remained for a week before making for Easter Island.

At the beginning of October, communication was received from *Dresden* advising that she was now in Pacific waters but was being trailed by two enemy cruisers *Good Hope* and *Monmouth* and on the 4th she was ordered to Easter Island to rendezvous with the rest of the squadron (*Leipzig* had already received instructions to head for this location with any coal that she had been able to obtain from American suppliers). Such signals were in no way secure and his message to *Dresden* was intercepted by the British wireless station at Suva. It was immediately relayed to the Admiralty in London, which issued the appropriate orders to Rear Admiral Sir Christopher Cradock, commander of the 4th Cruiser Squadron and the newly created (and ad hoc) South American Station, whose task was to protect British trade in the South Atlantic.

Unaware of these latest developments, von Spee arrived at the Easter Island rendezvous on 12 October, one day after *Dresden* and, two days later, *Leipzig* arrived with three laden colliers in tow. Although Easter Island belonged to Chile, its governor was actually an Englishman named Percy Edmonds who – without wireless communication to the outside world – was blissfully unaware of the outbreak of war and thus, believing the German ships to be on a routine cruise, was perfectly willing to supply them with whatever foodstuffs were available.

The German squadron would spend six days on Easter Island and, on 18 October, von Spee charted a course for the island of Más a Fuera a further 1,500 miles to the east, and only 450 miles from the coast of Chile. The island was reached on 26 October and a further three days were spent replenishing the ships' coal bunkers before the journey was resumed, the squadron steering for the port of Valparaiso where the admiral hoped to pick up much local intelligence and to relay further information to his superiors in Berlin.

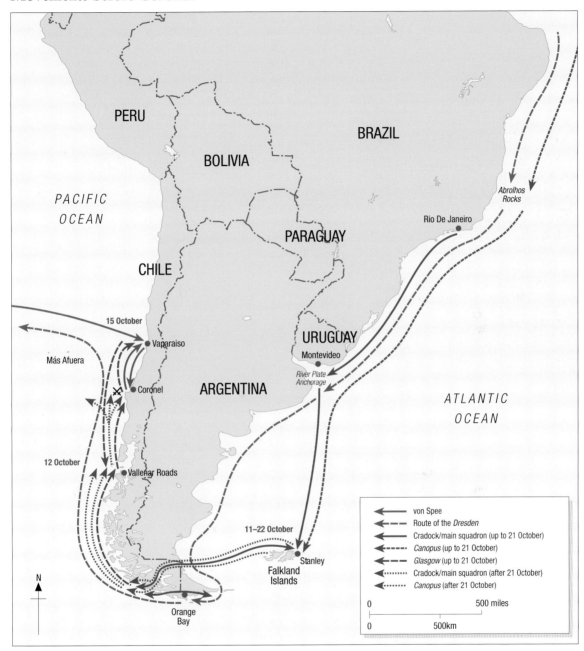

CORKING THE BOTTLE

The hunt for von Spee had been restricted before it had even begun. The local commanders, Jerram and Patey, were both of the opinion that the only priority for the allies was to protect the trade routes by seeking out and destroying potential threat, in this case posed by the East Asia Squadron. Their advice was ignored and during the planning for a future conflict, the Imperial General Staff in London gave instructions that absolute priority should be given to the provision of suitable escorts for troop convoys.

Therefore, when it became necessary for the ANZAC expeditionary force to sail for Europe, escorts were drawn from the East Indies Station, whilst Patey was ordered to cover the landings on German New Guinea and Samoa.

Quite simply the destruction of the enemy squadron was never seen as a priority and as a result, the German ships were able to conceal themselves in the vast expanse of the ocean whilst Australia, New Zealand and then Japan – who entered the war on 23 August – began what can only be construed as a premature dismemberment of the German colonial empire. Eventually in late September, when Patey in *Australia* with the French cruiser *Montcalm* as escort, were released to search for von Spee, their target was already 5,000 miles farther east. Before he could begin his pursuit, Patey was obliged to return to Rabaul in order to resupply. After leaving port on 2 October, he was refused permission to proceed any farther than Fiji. The strongest allied vessel in the Pacific had been relegated to patrolling local trade routes.

Britain's preoccupation with the protection of her maritime trade was understandable, for without the necessary raw materials she would be unable to raise and supply her armed forces. Therefore, when war broke out, the 4th Cruiser Squadron under Rear Admiral Sir Christopher Cradock – based

HMS *Carnarvon*. Stoddart's flagship, mechanical faults prevented *Carnarvon* from taking much part during the battle of the Falklands, her bad luck continuing during the search for *Dresden* when she ran aground and was badly holed. (IWM, Q003073)

on the American Station and consisting of four elderly light cruisers (*Berwick*, *Essex*, *Lancaster* and *Suffolk*) and the relatively modern *Bristol* – was immediately 'reinforced' by five obsolete armoured cruisers: *Carnarvon*, *Cornwall*, *Cumberland*, *Monmouth* and *Good Hope*, all of which had been withdrawn from units in British home waters as they were deemed unsuitable for a modern naval war.

Given the clamour for protection coming from the merchant navy, the Admiralty then took the decision to establish a South American Station, and divided Cradock's force to cover both areas. Appointed to this new command, he was given *Good Hope* and *Monmouth*, to which were added the modern light cruiser *Glasgow* and the armed liner *Otranto*. His brief was to protect merchant shipping in the South Atlantic whilst simultaneously seeking out and sinking *Dresden*. The threat posed by *Karlsruhe* was to be negated by Rear Admiral Archibald P. Stoddart, then in command of the Cape Verde/Canaries Station, whose forces would be augmented by *Carnarvon*, *Cornwall* and *Cumberland*. The remaining light cruisers were to continue with mercantile protection duties in the North Atlantic.

Cradock's appointment was a poisoned chalice – his 'ragtag' squadron unsuited to the task for which it was established but also, with the exception of Stanley in the Falkland Islands, was not only dependent on neutral countries for resupply. His only other options for receiving coal from friendly colliers were the Abrolhos Rocks, a group of rocky islets marking the edge of Brazilian territory, and a shallow area in the estuary of the River Plate.

Rear Admiral A. P. Stoddart, Commander of the RN Cape Verde/Canaries Station. (IWM, Q069172)

Of the ships themselves, only *Glasgow* could be deemed capable of the service required of her, whilst both *Good Hope* and *Monmouth* were manned by scratch crews drawn from the Naval Reserve and Coastguard. The final component of the squadron, the armed liner *Otranto*, would prove to be a liability, the only advantage to her presence being that she would allow Cradock to extend his line of search whilst looking for *Dresden*.

Moving methodically down the coast of South America, Cradock had perhaps his only stroke of luck – he fell in with the liner *Carmania* which carried a cargo of precious coal as well as other well needed supplies. Her captain elected to stay with Cradock's motley force and was sent to reconnoitre Trinidad Island, some 600 miles off the Brazilian coast. Here he encountered three German vessels, two of which made good their escape but the third – *Cap Trafalgar*, also an armed liner – initially tried to escape, then elected to stay and fight it out. At noon the *Carmania* opened fire and eventually *Cap Trafalgar* was sunk.

Carmania's part in the campaign was over and Cradock continued towards the Falklands, his main concern no longer the elusive *Dresden* but rather the whereabouts of her master, the even more elusive von Spee. On 5 September he sent a short message to the Admiralty: '*Gneisenau* and *Scharnhorst* spotted Caroline Islands on 8 August.... Is there any news as to their current whereabouts? Several German colliers reported in the vicinity of the Magellan Straits.' London was just as much in the dark as Cradock and could reply only that it was a possibility that the East Asia Squadron was indeed intent on entering the South Atlantic. In time, and in no doubt owing to the fact that neither Patey nor Jerram nor the Imperial Japanese Navy had, until then, been able to locate him, it became clear that in all probability the German admiral was indeed heading directly towards the ad hoc British squadron.

Almost immediately Cradock received new orders via the British Embassy in Rio:

THE DUEL OF THE ARMED LINERS: THE SHATTERED BRIDGE OF THE "CARMANIA" AFTER HER VICTORY OVER THE "CAP TRAFALGAR."

The armed liner "Carmania," in her hour and a-half's fight of September 14 with the German armed liner "Cap Trafalgar," was hit by 73 of her opponent's shells, the splinters making, it is stated, some 80 holes all over the vessel. Offering so large a target to gun-fire as did the "Carmania"—a ship of great length, standing 60 feet out of the water—she was saved from suffering more damage by the seamanship of Captain Noel Grant, R.N., her Captain, who kept her end-on to the enemy. Our photograph of the navigating bridge of the "Carmania," with the engine-room telegraphs wrecked and fragments of metal strewn about, will give an idea of what those on board went through. It has just reached this country.—[*Photo. by Farringdon Co.*]

Theoretically unsuited to combat, the deck of the RMS *Carmania* graphically shows the damage she received during the fight with the German steamer *Cap Trafalgar*. (Author's collection)

There is a strong possibility of *Scharnhorst* and *Gneisenau* arriving in the Magellan Straits or on the west coast of South America, where the Germans have much local trade…. Leave sufficient force in the Atlantic to deal with *Dresden* and *Karlsruhe*. Concentrate a squadron strong enough to meet *Scharnhorst* and *Gneisenau*, making the Falkland Islands your coaling base. *Canopus* [an outdated pre-dreadnought battleship] is en-route to meet you at Abrolhos whilst *Defence* [a relatively new, but still obsolete armoured cruiser] is joining you from the Mediterranean. Until *Defence* comes up keep at least *Canopus* and one 'County' class cruiser with your flagship and as soon as you have superior strength, be prepared to search the Magellan Straits, being ready to return and cover the River Plate or, depending on local information, search as far north as Valparaiso. Break up the German trade and destroy the German cruisers.

For a squadron manned mainly by reservists it was a tall order and, although certain aspects of the communiqué, such as how to concentrate his ships or where to make his forward base, were concise and straightforward, the actual instructions themselves are almost criminally ambiguous. The force commanded by Stoddart had been formed principally to meet the threat from *Dresden* and *Karlsruhe* and, with the former known to have left the South Atlantic, Cradock would have been operating fully within the remit of his orders if he had detached a number of ships from his colleague in order to reinforce his own squadron – there were but four County-class cruisers in the region of which three were operating under Stoddart's orders. If such a transfer hadn't been considered by the Admiralty, then the admonition for

Cradock to keep 'at least one "County" class cruiser' with his flagship makes no sense, as only one such vessel – *Monmouth* – was under his direct command. Yet there was always the fear that the enemy commander would evade this latest attempt to bring him to battle and, as Cradock blithely entered Pacific waters in what would become another fruitless search, would himself sail into the South Atlantic. With no credible reserve available to stop him, von Spee would have Britain's valuable trade routes at his mercy.

Tied to the slow-moving *Canopus*, the key to Cradock's plan of campaign now lay in the anticipated arrival of *Defence*, which, armed with four 9.2in. and ten 7.5in. guns, would have given him sufficient firepower to engage the Ostasiengeschwader. Assuming that she would be sailing from the Mediterranean at an average speed of 15kts, Cradock hoped that she would rendezvous with him during the early part of October and planned to hold her in reserve whilst *Monmouth*, *Glasgow* and *Otranto* conducted a reconnaissance in force around Cape Horn and the Magellan Straits. Some distance to the north, Stoddart would remain in a supporting position with his three armoured cruisers.

Although we cannot be certain, in the light of later events, a reasonable assumption would be that Cradock personally intended to oversee operations from the Falkland Islands, within easy communication at all times of the various elements of his command. Unknown to Cradock, his situation was to change dramatically on 14 September when von Spee made his abortive attempt to catch the New Zealand Expeditionary force at Apia on Samoa. Believing that the German squadron had continued on its north-westerly course, the Admiralty cancelled *Defence*'s sailing orders and she remained in

'The citadel under whose protection you will shelter.' The ageing battleship *Canopus* inflicted on Cradock by an Admiralty out of touch with the realities of the campaign. (IWM, Q038433)

The crew of *Good Hope* shortly before the onset of the campaign. (Coronel Memorial)

the Mediterranean. In their infinite wisdom, however, no one at naval headquarters saw fit to inform Cradock of this fundamental change in plans. Instead he received a communiqué which read: 'Situation changed, *Gneisenau* appeared off Samoa on the 14th and left steering NW. German trade on west coast of America is to be attacked at once. Cruisers need not be concentrated. Two cruisers and an armed liner appear sufficient for Magellan Straits and west coast. Advise what you propose to do about *Canopus*.'

Despite this last message from London, Cradock was convinced more than ever that the enemy were still heading for the Americas and, therefore, before leaving for the South Atlantic he sent a personal note to King George V, with whom he had earlier served. 'I have a feeling', he wrote, 'that the two heavy cruisers from China are making their way to the Straits of Magellan, and am just off there to see.' He also used the opportunity to reaffirm his concerns by sending a message to the Admiralty – via the British Consulate in Montevideo – to the effect that any and all intelligences received with regard to the movements and locations of any of von Spee's ships be communicated to him as a matter of priority.

Cradock's ships made their passage through the Cockburn Channel, dividing Cape Horn from the rest of Tierra del Fuego and, steaming into Orange Bay, they found no trace of *Dresden* save a carved tablet that confirmed her presence there during the first weeks of September. Running low on coal, and with the weather steadily worsening, Cradock had no other option than to return to the Falklands to refuel and resupply. It was now that a chance wireless interception seemed to indicate that *Dresden* was still hovering around the Magellan Straits; Cradock ordered *Glasgow*, *Monmouth* and *Otranto*, under the overall command of Captain John Luce, back into the Pacific with instructions to search as far north as Valparaiso. He would remain in Stanley, in order to maintain better wireless contact with the Admiralty in London.

As they rounded Cape Horn for the second time in a matter of days, the Royal Navy ships were battered and pounded by heavy seas and gale force winds. Eventually they rode out the storm and on 12 October reached the temporary coaling station at Vallenar. Having refuelled, Luce decided to leave *Otranto* behind and proceed farther with only *Monmouth* in company. Cradock's anxiety about a chance encounter with a superior German force was on everyone's mind, as Luce later wrote:

> It seemed to both the captain of *Monmouth* and myself that we were running a considerable risk without much object, and I should have preferred to have gone on ahead alone in *Glasgow*, which I knew to be faster than any ship in the German squadron. *Monmouth*, which had been long overdue for a refit could – at best – only match the Germans for speed, whilst her fighting value would not avail against their superior armoured cruisers.

Passing the small port of Coronel, the two British cruisers reached Valparaiso on 15 October, anchoring amidst a number of German steamers who immediately relayed this information to Berlin. Having found no trace of enemy warships the two cruisers then made ready to retrace their steps southwards, but their departure was delayed when *Monmouth* had to carry out some repairs to her overworked boilers.

With the reconnaissance under way, Cradock received another contradictory message: 'It appears that *Scharnhorst* and *Gneisenau* are working their way across to South America.... You must be prepared to meet them. *Canopus* should accompany *Glasgow*, *Monmouth* and *Otranto*, the ships to search and protect trade in combination.... If you propose that *Good Hope* should move to the west coast, then you should leave *Monmouth* on the east.'

Again, the Admiralty had issued orders that bore no resemblance to either the military situation or indeed the forces at Cradock's disposal. He was to seek out the enemy who – it was now admitted – could be the entire Ostasiengeschwader whilst simultaneously protecting British trade, and in his reply Cradock asked two rather probing questions of his superiors. Firstly he requested confirmation that *Defence*, which by now should at least have been in wireless contact with the squadron commander, was indeed being transferred to his command, and secondly he enquired about the policy of the Panama Canal Company regarding the transit of belligerent shipping. If permitted, von Spee could easily use the waterway as a short cut to enter an area of vital importance to Britain's maritime trade, whilst avoiding any blocking forces deployed by the Royal Navy. Although the American Government declined to give a direct answer to British enquiries, the prevalent opinion was that up to three belligerent ships could transit the canal at any one time. This would mean that both *Scharnhorst* and her consort, *Gneisenau*, could enter the Caribbean with either a light cruiser or auxiliary in company and then sail for the Atlantic to effect a rendezvous with *Karlsruhe*, which was then still operating off the Brazilian coast.

On 11 October, having received no response to his previous message, Cradock wrote again, this time pointing out the dangers of employing a single squadron to seek out and engage von Spee. He suggested that a second force be deployed not only to support the first, but also to act as a strategic reserve should the unthinkable happen and von Spee eluded this latest attempt by the Royal Navy to bring him to battle. His suggestion was that Luce would remain on the west coast with *Glasgow*, *Monmouth* and *Otranto* whilst an 'east coast squadron' based around his flagship *Good Hope* would consist of *Canopus* and *Defence*. Both of these were – as far as he had been advised by

A sister ship of *Monmouth*, *Kent* would aptly be responsible for the sinking of her nemesis – *Nürnberg*. (IWM, Q021415)

his superiors – still sailing to join his command along with the armoured cruiser *Cornwall* which would be detached from Stoddart's squadron according to Cradock's understanding of his initial orders.

Three days later, Cradock received London's response. Ominously his suggestion of creating an 'east coast squadron' was endorsed and he was advised that the new formation would comprise *Carnarvon* and *Cornwall*, the light cruiser *Bristol* – which would come south from the North American Station – the armed merchantmen *Macedonia* and *Orama* and finally *Defence*, once more on its way from the Mediterranean. This new squadron was to be commanded by a flag officer, as yet unnamed, but what was clear from the Admiralty communiqué was that the officer in question would definitely not be Cradock.

Regrettably we are unable to hear the opinions of Captains Philip Francklin and Frank Brandt of *Good Hope* and *Monmouth* respectively but their contemporary, John Luce, of *Glasgow* made no secret of his thoughts: 'There was not force available at the moment to form two squadrons of sufficient strength and speed and we should not have advanced into the Pacific until this was forthcoming, but [should] have concentrated in the Straits using the Falklands as a base.' Luce agreed with his commanding officer that British maritime trade on the western coast of South America was of such negligible value in times of war, that it would have been for the best if the ships remained in port until the rogue enemy squadron had been met and destroyed. Indeed as he was later to point out, that would have been the case in normal circumstances if insufficient escort vessels had been available.

Luce continued: 'Cradock seems to have thought, however, that the Admiralty were pressing him to attack and his ardent fighting spirit could not brook anything in the nature of defensive strategy.' Here we have the crucial factor, which ultimately led to Cradock's making for Coronel. It is clear that he was under the impression that he was to seek out and engage von Spee wherever he could be found, an opinion supported by the testimony of one of his most trusted and able lieutenants. Yet this was not the view in the corridors of Whitehall, the source of Cradock's operational instructions. The First Lord – Winston Churchill – was fatally to misread the situation when he forwarded Cradock's enquiry of 11 October to the First Sea Lord, Prince Louis von Battenberg with the following accompanying note: 'It would be best for the British ships to keep within supporting distance of each other, whether in the Straits or at the Falklands, and to postpone the cruise along the west coast until the present uncertainty about *Scharnhorst* and *Gneisenau* is cleared up.'

Over the course of the next few days, both Churchill and Battenberg were to compound matters by firstly instructing Cradock to concentrate the bulk of his squadron on the Falklands, whilst sending *Glasgow* to attack German trade on the west coast. Having by now agreed between themselves that should Cradock feel too weak to engage the enemy with any realistic chance of victory, he should merely attempt to shadow them, they then further complicated things by appointing Stoddart as 'Senior Naval Officer North of Montevideo', assigning him the reinforcements that Cradock required and desired. If this were not enough, Cradock was ordered to tie his squadron to *Canopus*, for in Churchill's own words she was 'a citadel around which all our cruisers in those waters could find absolute security'.

Owing to continuing engine trouble, the elderly battleship was slowly making her way to join the squadron, news that led Cradock to write once more to London, stressing in the cable the impossibility of his situation. Whilst reaffirming his intention of forcing an engagement whenever the enemy was found, he questioned the practicality of this plan when he would

This photograph of the British warships in heavy seas conveys the conditions in which Coronel was fought. (IWM, Q017997)

be limited to *Canopus'* best speed of 12kts whilst many of the German ships that he was fated to encounter could achieve almost double this. Churchill took his message to indicate his planned compliance with his existing orders.

Whilst stranded on the Falklands awaiting *Canopus'* arrival, Cradock was painfully aware that the rest of his squadron could encounter the enemy at any time and thus, when he was informed that she would require further repairs his patience snapped. He ordered *Good Hope* to make immediate preparations to put to sea whilst ordering *Canopus'* captain to make running repairs and then follow at his best possible speed whilst acting as escort to the squadron's three colliers. As the flagship left harbour at Stanley, a simple message was sent to the Admiralty: '*Good Hope* left 22 October via Cape Horn, *Canopus* following on 23 via Magellan Straits with three colliers for west coast of South America.'

CHRONOLOGY

1897 Admiral Alfred Tirpitz appointed head of the Reichsmarineamt.

German naval forces seize the port of Tsingtao.

1898 First German Naval Law enacted, a construction programme intended to bring the Imperial Navy in line with the navies of France and Russia.

1900 Second German Naval Law enacted.

Outbreak of the Boxer Rising in China.

1902 Treaty of Alliance signed between Great Britain and Japan.

1904 'Entente Cordiale' signed between France and Great Britain.

Outbreak of the Russo-Japanese War.

1905 Japan victorious at the battle of the Tsushima Straits.

Russia sues for peace.

1906 Third German Naval Law enacted.

Britain launches HMS *Dreadnought*, a revolutionary design that immediately renders all other battleships obsolete.

Germany enacts First Amendment to the Second Naval Law (1900).

1907 Triple Alliance signed between France, Great Britain and Russia.

Germany announces the creation of the Hochseestreitkräfte, her major naval formation for action in European waters.

1908 Germany enacts Second Amendment to the Second Naval Law.

Imperial Navy increases research into the development of submarines.

1910 Japan annexes Korea from China.

1912 Germany enacts Third Amendment to the Second Naval Law.

1914

20 June Von Spee sails from Tsingtao.

1 August Berlin issues the *Kriegsgefahr*.

5 August Britain declares war on Germany.

10–14 September *Emden* at large in Indian waters.

15 October *Glasgow* and *Monmouth* arrive at Valparaiso.

1 November Battle of Coronel.

8 December Battle of the Falkland Islands.

1915

14 March *Dresden* scuttled at Más a Tierra.

OPPOSING COMMANDERS

GERMAN COMMANDERS

Vizeadmiral Maximilian, Reichsgraf von Spee (1861–1914). Maximilian von Spee was born in Copenhagen on 22 June 1861, the fifth of nine children. He pursued a naval career which saw him spend his initial service in German West Africa where he remained until 1889 when he returned to Germany and married the Baroness Margarethe von der Osten-Sacken.

Over the next six years he rose through the ranks and placed his first true step on the ladder to senior command in December 1897 when he was transferred as flag officer to Vizeadmiral Otto von Diederichs, the newly promoted commander of the Ostasiengeschwader. Returning from the Far East, von Spee was promoted to *Korvettenkapitän*, as first officer of the battleship *Brandenburg*. After a number of further local commands, he was transferred to the Navy Office in Berlin as an expert in naval mines.

On 27 January 1904, he received his promotion to *Fregattenkapitän* and exactly one year later was advanced to *Kapitän zur See*, the final rung on the ladder to flag rank. With it came command of the battleship *Wittelsbach*, his last naval command, before being appointed Chief of Staff to the Baltic Fleet, in September 1908. On 27 January 1910, he was promoted to *Konteradmiral*.

In 1912, von Spee transferred to the Ostasiengeschwader. Although senior naval officer at Tsingtao, he was technically too low in rank to exercise the squadron command, a deficiency that was rectified in 1913 with his promotion to *Vizeadmiral*.

Korvettenkapitän Karl Friedrich Max von Müller (1873–1923). The son of a Prussian army officer, von Müller took advantage of the army's domination of the Imperial Navy to transfer into the junior service on Easter 1891, serving first on the training ship *Stosch* and then on the cruiser *Gneisenau*, namesake of the ship that would later serve with the Ostasiengeschwader, before transferring to the battleship *Baden* in October 1894 as signal lieutenant.

Receiving promotion to *Oberleutnant zur See*, von Müller was given command of the gunboat *Schwalbe*, assigned to protect German interests off the coast of East Africa, and it was here that he contracted the bout of malaria that would plague him for the rest of his life.

Invalided back to Germany, von Müller spent a number of years in various shore assignments before joining the battleship *Kaiser Wilhelm II*, flagship of the High Seas Fleet – the Hochseestreitkräfte – as second gunnery officer. It was a fateful appointment that would shape his future career as he soon came to the notice of Prince Henry of Prussia, the Kaiser's younger brother, who arranged for von Müller's appointment to his personal staff.

After several years' further service, von Müller received the coveted promotion to *Korvettenkapitän* in December 1908, transferring to the Reichsmarineamt in Berlin where he came to the notice of Grossadmiral Alfred von Tirpitz.

Early in 1913, he returned to active service, being given command of the light cruiser *Emden*, based at Tsingtao. On receipt of the notice of *Kriegsgefahr*, *Emden* left Tsingtao on the evening of 31 July and, four days later, captured the Russian mail packet *Ryazan*, the first prize to be captured by the Kaiserliche Marine during World War I, before rendezvousing with the remainder of the Ostasiengeschwader at Pagan Island.

During the autumn of 1913 *Emden* and her commander conducted a daring campaign in which they took 14 prizes whilst also bombarding the oil refinery at Madras and subsequently accounting for the Russian cruiser *Zhemchug* and the French destroyer *Mousquet* at the Malaysian port of Penang.

The German captain's luck ran out on 8 November. Whilst attempting to destroy an Allied radio station on the Keeling Islands, *Emden* was engaged by the Australian light cruiser *Sydney* and, after a long and hard-fought battle, was battered into submission. After his surrender, von Müller was interned on Malta and, in 1916, he was moved to a camp for officers near Nottingham and eventually repatriated to Germany in late 1918.

In recognition of his exploits, von Müller was promoted to *Kapitän zur See* and was awarded the *Pour le Mérite*, the coveted *Blue Max* before retiring from the navy on grounds of ill health, eventually succumbing to the effects of his long-term illness on 11 March 1923.

BRITISH COMMANDERS

Rear Admiral Sir Christopher G. F. M. Cradock, KCVO, CB (1862–1914). Having graduated from the Royal Naval Training Ship *Britannia*, Cradock saw varied initial service in both the Mediterranean and Channel fleets before being appointed as acting sub-lieutenant on the corvette *Cleopatra* on the China Station, a promotion that was confirmed in March 1883.

Cradock's progress over the next decade was steady and, in 1896, he was appointed to the command of the light cruiser *Alacrity* on the China Station shortly before the outbreak of the Boxer Rising, and in the summer of 1899 he was given command of a mixed assault force that spearheaded the Western

Powers' attack on the Taku Forts, the first stage in their attempt to relieve the beleaguered western enclaves in Peking. The Chinese Intervention would prove to be a significant turning point in Cradock's career, as in June 1902, he was knighted. Within a year he was commanding *Bacchante*, a cruiser serving with the Mediterranean Fleet, before transferring to the pre-dreadnought *Swiftsure*, a remarkably fast, but by British standards lamentably under-armed battleship. Cradock's previous service was noted when on 1 July 1909 he was appointed Commodore, Second Class, in command of the Royal Naval Barracks in Portsmouth and in August 1910, Cradock was promoted Rear Admiral.

Further promotion came in August 1911 when he joined the Atlantic Fleet as deputy to Vice Admiral Sir John Jellicoe, taking command of the 3rd Battle Squadron. On 12 December 1911, he was ordered to assist the P&O steamer *Delhi* which had foundered in heavy seas off the coast of Morocco. The Duke of Fife, the King's brother-in-law, was amongst those taken safely off the wreck; he contracted a fatal bout of pleurisy during his ordeal and Cradock felt that many, including Winston Churchill, unfairly blamed him for the Duke's subsequent death. It was a cloud that would remain over him until the fateful engagement at Coronel.

In February 1912 Cradock was made a Knight Commander of the Victorian Order and appointed commander of the North American and West Indian Station, based on Bermuda. This was all to change however on 8 February 1913 when, having raised his flag on *Suffolk*, Cradock received a message from the Admiralty transferring the strategic direction of his command to the First Fleet. That said, the change had no real effect as, to all intents and purposes, the ships remained on detachment in American waters, to observe British interests in Mexico. With the outbreak of war, Cradock's force was reinforced by the transfer of four elderly armoured cruisers from the Reserve Fleet (*Carnarvon*, *Cornwall*, *Cumberland* and *Monmouth*), whilst a fifth vessel – *Good Hope* – was transferred from the Grand Fleet at Scapa Flow.

Events would soon overtake him, and within two months of the commencement of hostilities, Cradock was en route to South American waters, to meet the challenge of von Spee's East Asia Squadron.

Vice Admiral Sir Frederick Doveton Sturdee, GCB, KCMG, CVO (1859–1925). Born into a family with strong naval ties, it was inevitable that Sturdee would follow his forbears and enlist in the 'Senior Service'. And so in 1871, after attending the Royal Naval School, New Cross, he joined the training ship *Britannia*. Within two years the young cadet had been promoted to midshipman serving both in the Channel Fleet and then on the East India Station before returning as a sub-lieutenant to the gunnery school at HMS *Excellent* where he studied for two years before receiving his lieutenancy.

In 1880 the newly promoted Lieutenant Sturdee joined the Mediterranean Fleet, taking part in the Egyptian campaign, before returning once more to Great Britain for training in the use and deployment of torpedoes, and after a short period of further active service returned to the Torpedo School as an instructor. In 1893 Sturdee was promoted to commander and transferred to the Admiralty, becoming Director of Naval Ordnance. After four years in this position he transferred to the Australia Station where, in 1899, after mediating between America and Germany in a territorial dispute over the Samoan Islands, he received his promotion to captain and was awarded the CMG.

Returning again to London, Sturdee served initially as assistant to the Director of Naval Intelligence, before his appointment as Chief of Staff, Mediterranean Fleet. Receiving the CVO in 1906 he then took command of the battle cruiser *New Zealand* before becoming Chief of Staff, Channel Fleet. In 1910 he received his promotion to Rear Admiral, assuming command of the 1st Battle Squadron, before a short stint as chair of the Admiralty Submarine Committee, and then a return to the Home Fleet as Commanding Admiral (Cruisers).

His star steadily rising, Sturdee was created KCB in June 1913, and with promotion to Vice Admiral before the year was out it seemed as if the rise would continue with his further promotion to Chief of the War Staff, directly subordinate to the then First Sea Lord, Prince Louis von Battenburg. However, the outbreak of war led to a wave of anti-German hysteria in Great Britain, and Battenburg was hounded out of office, his place being taken by Sir John Fisher, the Royal Navy's *enfant terrible*. It looked as if Sturdee's career was over, given the personal antipathy between him and Fisher, until the fateful news of Coronel was received in London. Then he was found to be the closest officer of suitable rank and seniority to assume command of Britain's counterstroke in the wake of Coronel.

OPPOSING PLANS

GERMAN PLANS

Given the divided nature of the Imperial Navy's higher command structure, and the simple fact that the focus of attention had lain – from its inception – with the High Seas Fleet, the Hochseestreitkräfte, little actual thought had been given to the future actions of the Ostasiengeschwader once the fighting had started. This was despite the preparations undertaken to ensure that all arms of the German military were prepared for the inevitable outbreak of hostilities.

Standing orders advocated the adoption of cruiser warfare – the *guerre de course* – but this tactic was rendered both unsuitable and unrealistic by the presence of the very two vessels that made the East Asia Squadron such a formidable proposition: the armoured cruisers *Scharnhorst* and *Gneisenau*. Given the overwhelming Allied superiority in theatre, Berlin agreed to give von Spee the utmost discretion over his actions, and it was the admiral himself who decided for both military and logistical reasons to keep his force intact whilst detaching a single vessel, *Emden*, to the Indian Ocean.

Von Spee's actions as his squadron progressed across the Pacific Ocean were dictated by the limited intelligence available to him and, of course, by events as they unfolded. Ultimately his plan was to cause as much damage to the enemy as possible, for as long as possible. However, the destruction of Cradock's force at Coronel made the chance to return to German waters a real possibility. Therefore, in the wake of the battle the Imperial High Command was divided between interfering in what had been, up to that point, a successful strategy by ordering von Spee to return directly to Germany, where a sortie by the High Seas Fleet, would cover his final movements, and continuing to allow the admiral to act on his own discretion, on the tactical rather than the strategic situation. In the final analysis, it was this lack of firm direction from his superiors in Berlin that contributed to the delays after Coronel which later combined to cause von Spee to lose the race to the Falkland Islands, forcing him into an unavoidable battle on unfavourable terms.

BRITISH PLANS

Like their opposite numbers in Berlin, at the outbreak of war, the Lords of the Admiralty in London were fully occupied with many concerns, none of which actually centred on the conduct or neutralization of the Ostasiengeschwader.

In short there was a list of global priorities that needed to be met before any other operations could be considered. Therefore on the commencement of hostilities, the Standing Orders of the Imperial General Staff dictated that the navy give *absolute* priority to the escort of the various expeditionary forces – The BEF from Britain to France, a force from India to German East Africa and, crucially, the ANZAC forces sent to occupy German possessions on New Guinea and the Bismarck Archipelago.

As a result of these conditions, the Allied ships were inevitably relegated to searching for a needle in a haystack, despite their overwhelming superiority in numbers, and the Admiralty was forced to dispatch a scratch formation, based upon Cradock's 4th Cruiser Squadron in an attempt to defeat the German force. However, not only were Cradock's ships, in the main, obsolete in comparison with the more modern enemy vessels, but erratic direction and contradictory orders from Whitehall served only to hamper the campaign from the outset, leading to a complete misinterpretation of both the tactical and strategic situation. It was a combination that, in conjunction with Cradock's own anxieties and misgivings, would force his hand and ultimately commit him to battle at Coronel.

The shock of this defeat, the first to be suffered by the Royal Navy in over a century, and the negative implications that it held for Britain's 'senior service' only served to galvanize her leaders into action and engender a need for revenge. It ensured that Britain's response would be swift, and laconically simple – to find von Spee, wherever he might be and to destroy him. All that had been denied to Cradock was now lavished upon Sturdee by the Admiralty. However, ships alone do not win battles and the initial deployments, as directed by Winston Churchill, signally failed to ensure that the required overwhelming force would be deployed to accomplish the task in hand. It was therefore left to the mercurial 'Jacky' Fisher, the First Sea Lord, to override the protests of his subordinates and ensure that three of the much-vaunted battle cruisers, *Invincible*, *Inflexible* and *Princess Royal* were detached from the Grand Fleet to bolster the forces already en route to the South Atlantic.

If Cradock had been rushed by his superiors into a tactical disadvantage, Sturdee was, in comparison, allowed to proceed as he saw fit. The unconscious delays that this would bring to his planning almost caused disaster which was averted only when John Luce of *Glasgow* persuaded him to leave the Abrolhos Rocks earlier than originally planned.

In short, whilst the adage states that 'no plan survives first contact', it is clear that the German 'reactive' strategy, in giving von Spee complete latitude, paid dividends both during the initial part of the campaign which culminated in his victory at Coronel and also in von Müller's independent cruise in the Indian Ocean. Whilst on the opposing side, the Admiralty's insistence on almost micromanaging Cradock can be directly attributable to his defeat, whereas the leeway given to Sturdee, a methodical rather than aggressive commander, almost led to a potentially worse disaster that was averted primarily owing to Fisher's interference in Churchill's deployments and Luce's insistence that his commanding admiral not delay in sailing for the Falklands.

OPPOSING FORCES

THE GERMAN EAST ASIA SQUADRON – DIE OSTASIENGESCHWADER

With von Tirpitz's focus on developing a battle fleet, the sole purpose of which was to engage the Royal Navy in home waters, it was natural that German warships serving overseas would lack the cachet and glamour of the Hochseestreitkräfte. However, with the development of the colony of Tsingtao – itself a microcosm of Germany – and with the majority of the Reich's colonial possessions being situated in the Western Pacific, it became inevitable that a naval force would soon be stationed there.

From the time of its establishment, the Ostasiengeschwader was viewed as a prestige appointment. Its vessels were perhaps not the most modern in the Kaiserliche Marine – both *Scharnhorst* and *Gneisenau* were amongst the last of their type to be built – nonetheless it was a highly drilled, elite unit, led by capable officers. Its ships proved their worth both in peacetime with their superlative performance in the annual Kaiser's Cup and in wartime with their conduct in victory and defeat at both Coronel and the Falklands.

At the commencement of hostilities, the principal vessels (excluding gunboats, torpedo boats etc.) of the Ostasiengeschwader were as follows:

SMS *Scharnhorst* – Kapitän zur See Felix Schultz (Flagship)
Completed: 1907, Complement: 765
Max Displacement 12,781 tons, Main Armour Belt: 6–6.75in., Designed Speed: 22.5kts
Length: 450ft, Beam: 71ft, Draught: 25ft
Main Armament: 8 x 8.2in., 6 x 5.9in., Broadside: 1,958lb, Max Range: 13,500yd

SMS *Gneisenau* – Kapitän zur See Gustav Märker
Completed: 1907, Complement: 765
Max Displacement 12,781 tons, Main Armour Belt: 6–6.75in., Designed Speed: 22.5kts
Length: 450ft, Beam: 71ft, Draught: 25ft
Main Armament: 8 x 8.2in., 6 x 5.9in., Broadside: 1,958lb, Max Range: 13,500yd

SMS *Nürnberg* – Kapitän zur See Karl von Schönberg
Completed: 1908, Complement: 322
Max Displacement 4,002 tons, Main Armour Belt: 0.75–2in., Designed Speed: 23kts
Length: 387ft, Beam: 44ft, Draught: 18ft
Main Armament: 10 x 4.1in., Broadside: 192lb, Max Range: 10,500yd

SMS *Leipzig* – Fregattenkapitän Johann Siegfried Haun

Completed: 1906, Complement: 303

Max Displacement 3,756 tons, Main Armour Belt: 0.75–2in., Designed Speed: 22kts

Length: 363ft, Beam: 43ft, Draught: 17.5ft

Main Armament: 10 x 4.1in., Broadside: 192lb, Max Range: 10,500yd

SMS *Dresden* – Kapitän zur See Fritz Emil Lüdecke

Completed: 1908, Complement: 361

Max Displacement 4,268 tons, Main Armour Belt: 0.75–2in., Designed Speed: 24kts

Length: 387ft, Beam: 44ft, Draught: 18ft

Main Armament: 10 x 4.1in, Broadside: 192lb, Max Range: 10,500yd

THE BRITISH 4TH CRUISER SQUADRON

Cradock's force was singularly unsuited to the task that it had been given, in effect being drawn from what was a largely ceremonial deployment and thrust into the hunt for a superior – in virtually every sense – enemy formation. Because of restrictions imposed by the War Plan of the Imperial General Staff, this group of largely obsolete vessels, of which the main elements could fight their full armament only in calm weather conditions and of which only *Glasgow* could be classed as the equal of any of von Spee's ships.

This incongruity in the composition of his squadron, as well as the fact that Cradock had to sail almost halfway across the globe in order to engage the enemy, hampered by a stream of contradictory orders from London, all combined to prevent him from achieving any form of unit integrity; factors that proved to be so beneficial to the opposing squadron.

Although the composition of his force changed several times during his passage from American waters, Cradock's force at Coronel comprised the following vessels:

HMS *Good Hope* – Captain Philip Francklin (Flagship)

Completed: 1902, Complement: 900

Max Displacement 14,100 tons, Main Armour Belt: 5–6in., Designed Speed: 23kts

Length: 530ft, Beam: 71ft, Draught: 28ft

Main Armament: 2 x 9.2in., 16 x 6in., Broadside: 1,560lb, Max Range: 12,500yd

HMS *Monmouth* – Captain Frank Brandt

Completed: 1903, Complement: 690

Max Displacement 9,800 tons, Main Armour Belt: 4–5in., Designed Speed: 23kts

Length: 463ft, Beam: 66ft, Draught: 25.5ft

Main Armament: 14 x 6in., Broadside: 900lb, Max Range: 11,200yd

HMS *Glasgow* – Captain John Luce

Completed: 1910, Complement: 411

Max Displacement 5,300 tons, Main Armour Belt: 0.75–2in., Designed Speed: 25kts

Length: 453ft, Beam: 47ft, Draught: 15.5ft

Main Armament: 2 x 6in., 10 x 4in., Broadside: 425lb, Max Range: 11,200yd

AMC *Otranto* – Captain Ernest W. Davidson

Completed: 1909, Complement: 350

Max Displacement 12,124 tons, Main Armour Belt: N/A, Designed Speed: 18kts
Length: 535ft, Beam: 64ft, Draught: 38ft
Main Armament: 4 x 4.7in., Broadside: N/A, Max Range: 10,000yd

THE BRITISH SOUTH ATLANTIC STATION

The defeat at Coronel sent tremors through the British High Command. Whilst it was clear that von Spee had to be brought to battle and destroyed it was also clear that the Admiralty's insistence on dividing its forces in the South Atlantic into a number of autonomous commands had simply denied Cradock the services of a number of warships, the presence of which at the earlier battle might have tipped the balance in Britain's favour and allowed him to neutralize a number of the German light cruisers which were indispensible to von Spee for gathering intelligence.

Aware that the remaining ships on station were now inferior to the German squadron, the Admiralty endorsed the transfer of a single battle cruiser to the South Atlantic to act as the flagship of a reconstituted squadron. In the eyes of Admiral Sir John Fisher, however, this was insufficient and instead he sent two battle cruisers to form the core of the new formation whilst a third was sent to cover the approaches to the Caribbean.

At the time many officers complained of Fisher's interference. However, in hindsight, sticking to his maxim of using overwhelming force, and deciding to override his colleague, Winston Churchill's plan of operations proved to be the correct course; combined, the enemy armoured cruisers might have proved to have been equal to a single battle cruiser.

In November–December 1914, the vessels under Sturdee's command were as follows:

HMS *Invincible* – Captain Tufton H. P. Beamish (Flagship)
Completed: 1908, Complement: 837
Max Displacement 20,000 tons, Main Armour Belt: 6–10in., Designed Speed: 25kts
Length: 567ft, Beam: 79ft, Draught: 26ft
Main Armament: 8 x 12in., 14 x 6in., Broadside: 6,800lb, Max Range: 16,400yd

HMS *Inflexible* – Captain Richard F. Phillimore
Completed: 1908, Complement: 837
Max Displacement 20,000 tons, Main Armour Belt: 6–10in., Designed Speed: 28kts
Length: 567ft, Beam: 79ft, Draught: 26ft
Main Armament: 8x 12in., 14 x 6in., Broadside: 6,800lb, Max Range: 16,400yd

HMS *Carnarvon* – Captain Harry L. d'E. Skipwith (Flagship Rear Adm. Stoddart)
Completed: 1905, Complement: 653
Max Displacement 10,850 tons, Main Armour Belt: 4.5–6in., Designed Speed: 22kts
Length: 474ft, Beam: 69ft, Draught: 26ft
Main Armament: 4 x 7.5in., 6 x 6in., Broadside: 1,100lb, Max Range: 12,000yd

HMS *Cornwall* – Captain Walter M. Ellerton
Completed: 1904, Complement: 690
Max Displacement 9,800 tons, Main Armour Belt: 4–5in., Designed Speed: 24kts
Length: 464ft, Beam: 66ft, Draught: 26ft
Main Armament: 14 x 6in., Broadside: 900lb, Max Range: 11,200yd

HMS *Kent* – Captain John D. Allen

Completed: 1903, Complement: 690

Max Displacement 9,800 tons, Main Armour Belt: 4–5in., Designed Speed: 24kts

Length: 464ft, Beam: 66ft, Draught: 26ft

Main Armament: 14 x 6in., Broadside: 900lb, Max Range: 11,200yd

HMS *Canopus* – Captain Heathcote S. Grant

Completed: 1900, Complement: 750

Max Displacement: 13,150 tons, Main Armour Belt: 6in., Designed Speed: 18kts

Length: 418ft, Beam: 74ft, Draught: 27ft

Main Armament: 4 x 12in., 12 x 6in., Broadside: 4,000lb, Max Range: 13,500yd

HMS *Bristol* – Captain Lewis Clinton-Baker

Completed: 1910, Complement: 411

Max Displacement: 4,800 tons, Main Armour Belt: 0.75–2in., Designed Speed: 27kts

Length: 453ft, Beam: 47ft, Draught: 15.5ft

Main Armament: 2 x 6in., 10 x 4in., Broadside: 425lb, Max Range: 11,200yd

THE CAMPAIGN

THE BATTLE OF CORONEL

Like many battles throughout history, the action at Coronel was brought about by a combination of faulty intelligence and simple bad luck on the part of one of the combatants. On 29 October, with his squadron steaming northwards along the Chilean coast, Cradock ordered Captain Luce in *Glasgow* to sail into the port of Coronel in order to collect any communications waiting at the British Consulate. Because of inadequate wireless coverage, messages from the Admiralty in London to vessels in South American waters were normally sent first of all as cables to Montevideo in Uruguay. From there they were relayed to the Falkland Islands and then retransmitted to ships at sea. Unfortunately for Cradock, he had not received them because of a combination of factors: Chilean government policy, poor atmospheric conditions and the sheer mountainous bulk of the Andes. Therefore, after leaving the Falklands Cradock's only method of relaying and collecting information or receiving orders was to send a ship into nearby ports at regular intervals in the hope that instructions or intelligence might be awaiting collection.

Produced to commemorate the 90th anniversary of the battle, these postage stamps show all of the main warships involved during the two stages of the battle. (Author's collection)

It was at this time that *Glasgow* intercepted a number of signals between a German warship – soon to be positively identified as the light cruiser

Leipzig – and a number of German merchantmen and when this information was relayed to Cradock on *Good Hope*, he had every reason to believe that he would soon be able to move on Coronel and engage a lone enemy vessel with his entire force. What he had no way of knowing, however, was that in order to mislead any Allied observers von Spee had been deliberately using *Leipzig* as a conduit for all wireless traffic for his ships and that the whole Ostasiengeschwader was at that time waiting just to the south of Valparaiso.

Meanwhile, within the port itself, *Glasgow*'s arrival had been observed by the German steamer *Göttingen* and her captain dutifully relayed this information to von Spee, who intended to bring the remaining ships of his squadron to link up with *Leipzig*, sharing Cradock's mistaken belief that he would shortly be attacking a single enemy cruiser with overwhelming force.

As his ships steamed southwards to what von Spee believed would be no more than a routine encounter, he made his dispositions – *Scharnhorst* and the light cruisers would position themselves to block the northern approaches to the port whilst *Gneisenau* would cover the Boca Chica island and channel farther to the north in case the British cruiser managed to evade the main German force. If the port authorities refused to act as von Spee expected, and force *Glasgow* to leave the port, one of the light cruisers would be detailed to sail into the port and insist upon compliance. It was a sensible plan, but the need to overhaul a number of merchantmen leaving the port meant that von Spee's ships were scattered at a time when concentration was imperative for the plan to succeed. In any event von Spee's concerns were irrelevant as *Glasgow* had already slipped out of Coronel during the early hours of the morning without waiting for either the German admiral or the Chilean authorities to make their wishes known.

Cradock's options, when *Glasgow* rejoined the squadron at 1200hrs on 1 November, were quite different. With the limited intelligence available to him, and with his force some 50 miles to the west of the port, the only definite factor was that *Leipzig* was somewhere to the north of Coronel. Almost two hours of precious time were lost while Cradock considered his options and, at 1350hrs, as he had only the vaguest idea of the German cruiser's location, he decided to deploy his ships in an extended line on an axis NE by E, with a distance of some 15 miles between each vessel. The plan was that, when the enemy ship had been spotted, the squadron would concentrate upon the ship that had made the positive identification and close for action. Closest inshore was *Glasgow*, with the armed merchantman *Otranto* coming next and then the armoured cruiser *Monmouth* extending the line out to sea, which was then closed by Cradock himself in *Good Hope*.

As the Royal Navy squadron steered its northward course the weather began to deteriorate steadily and so, running with gale force winds at his back and with the waves getting increasingly higher, Cradock gave the order for those vessels with side-mounted guns to seal their lower casemates and open the gun positions a little above the ship's waterline. It, of course, meant that both *Good Hope* and *Monmouth* would be unable to 'fight' with their full batteries, but the British admiral was expecting to encounter only a solitary enemy cruiser. He also felt that this relative reduction in firepower was a reasonable price to pay to ensure that his ships wouldn't take on water unnecessarily, thus adversely affecting their performance and raising the possibility of the lower decks becoming flooded. Then, at 1620hrs – and before the search line had been able to shake itself out into the prescribed

One of von Spee's three light cruisers, *Leipzig*'s presence at Coronel proved to be the catalyst leading to Britain's first naval defeat in almost a century. (Author's collection)

S. M. S. **Leipzig** wurde am 8. Dez. 1914 bei den Falklands-Inseln (Südamerika) durch mehrfache feindliche Übermacht angegriffen und nach heldenhafter Gegenwehr zum Sinken gebracht.

intervals – *Glasgow* spotted a column of smoke on the northern horizon, off his starboard bow, and altered course to investigate further.

Steadily forging his way southwards through the rough seas, Fregattenkapitän Haun of *Leipzig* was performing a similar task for the Ostasiengeschwader and, at a little after 1630hrs, the leading vessels of the opposing squadrons were able to positively identify the enemy vessel for which they were searching, and soon signals were being sent back to the two admirals – to Cradock, that *Leipzig* had been identified and to von Spee that *Glasgow* had been found. Both men then began to issue their final orders, orders which anticipated an easy engagement in which numbers and superior firepower would quickly settle the issue. As the minutes passed and the two formations closed with each other, reports began to come in from lookouts on the leading ships as they began to discern first one additional column of smoke, and then others until it was clear to both commanders that, instead of the anticipated limited action, a major engagement was about to take place.

For Cradock, the situation must have been an agonizing one. He had long held the belief that his dispatch to the South Atlantic with a force that was frankly inadequate to the task for which had been sent, was an act of Churchillian revenge for the *Delhi* debacle. Now the worst had come to pass, for a few miles distant – and closing – lay von Spee's crack squadron which, by any rational calculations, was far superior to his own command. At this time, and with the two forces still relatively distant from each other, he still had time to refuse battle and pull away. However, in doing so, he would most likely condemn the slow-moving *Otranto* to almost certain capture or sinking unless, of course, she could maintain a sufficient distance between her and the German cruisers until night fell.

There would have been no dishonour in disengagement, as Cradock would have been acting fully in accord with the most recent Admiralty orders, and pulling back to *Canopus* some 300 miles to the south would have greatly enhanced his firepower, albeit at the cost of slowing down the squadron and involving the two merchantmen sailing with the battleship in an action where their presence could serve only to compromise any battle plan. There was, however, another equally important consideration that he needed to factor into his final decision; Cradock knew that however inferior his own ships might be in comparison with the German squadron, von Spee had traversed the Pacific Ocean having successfully evaded all attempts to find him and bring him to battle. Now his squadron was the only unit available – British or Allied – that had the remotest chance of barring his egress into the South Atlantic, where the whole procedure would have to be repeated, this time with the rich Atlantic shipping lanes at the German admiral's mercy.

The cold truth was that he had no other choice and it would indeed have been out of character for Cradock to have made any other decision than to engage. If he could inflict sufficient damage upon either *Scharnhorst* or her consort then the necessity of her putting into a neutral port for repairs would not only pinpoint her position for the Admiralty, but would also give him time to realign the search for the German squadron and redeploy additional forces to bring the enemy to battle. Therefore at around 1700hrs he ordered all ships to concentrate on *Glasgow* and deploy into line-ahead, with *Good Hope* forming the head of the line followed by *Monmouth*, *Glasgow* and, finally, *Otranto*, his aim being to close the distance with the enemy as quickly as was possible in order to bring the squadron's principal armament, the 6in. guns, into effective range whereby he would have some chance of inflicting damage upon the enemy.

Cradock's decision to include *Otranto* in his line of battle has puzzled historians ever since that fateful day in November 1914. Indeed after the battle, *Glasgow*'s gunnery officer would write: 'We all thought that he would leave the *Otranto*... but perhaps he did not like leaving her to look after herself... she is such an enormous bulk that she can be seen for miles on the darkest night.' With only four 4.7in. guns, and with her maximum speed reduced to 16kts in the heavy swell, the merchantman was undoubtedly more of a liability than an asset to the British squadron. However by this stage, having identified an opposing force of only three German cruisers, it is possible that Cradock perhaps believed that the apparent presence of four British warships would give his adversary more pause for thought than if he

Cradock's flagship, the ill-fated *Good Hope*, initially believed to have escaped the battle but ultimately lost with all hands at Coronel. (IWM, Q021927)

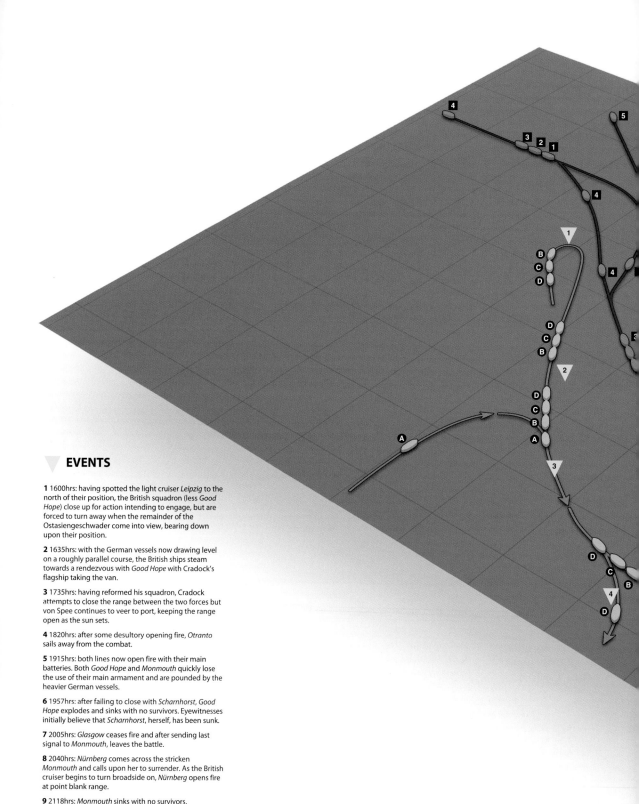

EVENTS

1 1600hrs: having spotted the light cruiser *Leipzig* to the north of their position, the British squadron (less *Good Hope*) close up for action intending to engage, but are forced to turn away when the remainder of the Ostasiengeschwader come into view, bearing down upon their position.

2 1635hrs: with the German vessels now drawing level on a roughly parallel course, the British ships steam towards a rendezvous with *Good Hope* with Cradock's flagship taking the van.

3 1735hrs: having reformed his squadron, Cradock attempts to close the range between the two forces but von Spee continues to veer to port, keeping the range open as the sun sets.

4 1820hrs: after some desultory opening fire, *Otranto* sails away from the combat.

5 1915hrs: both lines now open fire with their main batteries. Both *Good Hope* and *Monmouth* quickly lose the use of their main armament and are pounded by the heavier German vessels.

6 1957hrs: after failing to close with *Scharnhorst*, *Good Hope* explodes and sinks with no survivors. Eyewitnesses initially believe that *Scharnhorst*, herself, has been sunk.

7 2005hrs: *Glasgow* ceases fire and after sending last signal to *Monmouth*, leaves the battle.

8 2040hrs: *Nürnberg* comes across the stricken *Monmouth* and calls upon her to surrender. As the British cruiser begins to turn broadside on, *Nürnberg* opens fire at point blank range.

9 2118hrs: *Monmouth* sinks with no survivors.

THE BATTLE OF CORONEL, 1 NOVEMBER 1914

Cradock's squadron is destroyed by the Ostasiengeschwader.

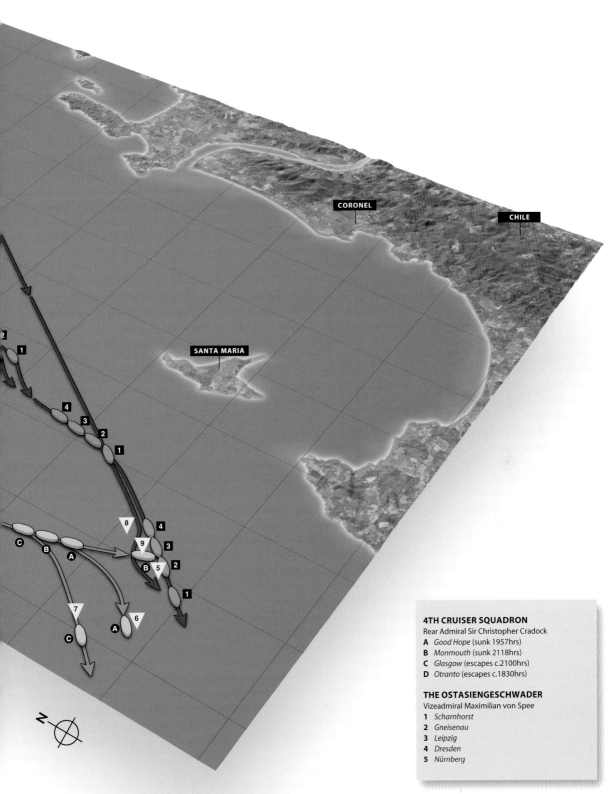

CORONEL

CHILE

SANTA MARIA

4TH CRUISER SQUADRON
Rear Admiral Sir Christopher Cradock
A *Good Hope* (sunk 1957hrs)
B *Monmouth* (sunk 2118hrs)
C *Glasgow* (escapes c.2100hrs)
D *Otranto* (escapes c.1830hrs)

THE OSTASIENGESCHWADER
Vizeadmiral Maximilian von Spee
1 *Scharnhorst*
2 *Gneisenau*
3 *Leipzig*
4 *Dresden*
5 *Nürnberg*

considered that the two forces were equal in number. It was also the case that *Otranto* was larger than *Canopus* and, in the failing light, her bulk might be mistaken for the antiquated battleship, the only vessel under Cradock's command that could conceivably give von Spee cause for concern. Whatever the truth of the matter, the fact that she was included in the British plan of engagement served to compromise the very plan of which she was an integral part as – in one of his final signals – the admiral betrayed his concerns about her possible fate when he said 'I cannot go down and engage the enemy at present (not without) leaving *Otranto*.'

To the north, von Spee was wrestling with a different set of emotions than his British counterpart – his tactics of misinformation and rapid movement had by now paid the dividends that he had anticipated; he had, to date, successfully avoided all enemy attempts at locating his force and now that his whereabouts had been discovered, he was in a position to destroy the only British ships capable of barring his further progress onto the final leg of his odyssey. Whether it would take him home to Germany or across to the coast of Africa remained uncertain; the immediate task in hand was to brush aside the enemy squadron and make passage for Cape Horn from where his ships would once more sail in the open waters, the sheer scale of which would once again serve to shield him from prying eyes.

By roughly 1700hrs, *Leipzig* had positively identified three of the British ships – at this time *Good Hope* was still out of sight, albeit steaming eastwards to reunite with the rest of her squadron; von Spee, encouraged by his overall superiority in numbers, ordered *Nürnberg* and *Dresden* to rejoin their consorts and he gave the order for the Ostasiengeschwader to attack the enemy. In the admiral's own words the squadron 'steamed at full speed in pursuit, keeping the enemy four points to starboard. The wind was south, force six, with a corresponding high sea, so that I had to be careful not to be manoeuvred into a lee position.' His intent was plainly to maintain a position between the British squadron and the Chilean coastline, where the darkening horizon would soon serve to obscure his ships' silhouettes and reduce the accuracy of the enemy guns whilst, conversely, the British cruisers would be held in stark relief against the setting sun. Making 14kts through the rough seas, von Spee ordered all boilers to be lit and for his ships to work their speed up to 20kts as quickly as possible.

According to another German account of the battle, von Spee then signalled his ships to engage the enemy, and rather than forming line they simply turned their bows starboard and with their captains calling for more speed, like hounds let off the leash, they bore down upon Cradock's formation:

> The water broke foaming over their bows as the vessels turned and raced on over the sea... it surged right over their forecastles. The German ships shuddered under the heavy thudding of their engines, the smoke pouring out of their funnels in thick, heavy, swathes which streamed like pennants behind the squadron.... The minutes flew by, one after another, until it became clear that they were gaining upon the enemy. At 17.50, with the wild chase having already lasted over an hour, another British ship was sighted. This would prove to be the '*Good Hope*' who placed herself at the head of the British line, the two rival squadrons now steaming towards each other on almost parallel southerly courses, their battle ensigns snapping bravely in the wind, and as the sun began to sink, a blood-red ball of fire in the west, the fight began.

At 1804hrs, Cradock, fully aware of the German vessels' superior firepower (an advantage that had been increased by the necessity of sealing a number of gun positions on the mess-decks of both *Good Hope* and *Monmouth*), signalled a change of course of four points to port, which would bring him closer to the enemy. He also hoped it would place his ships between the sun and the enemy, for a while at least blinding the German gunners but by now it must have been clear to him that his time was limited and that if he couldn't close with the opposing ships and quickly force an engagement, any combat would be strictly on the enemy's terms. Therefore he ordered all ships to increase speed to 17kts whilst sending a second signal to *Otranto* instructing her to proceed at her best possible speed and, with that, a rupture in the British line became inevitable. As his ships worked up to the desired speed, Cradock then ordered a message to be sent to *Canopus*, informing her captain, Heathcote Grant, of his position and telling him that battle was about to be joined. Grant informed the admiral of his own position, still some 250 miles to the south, advising him that, owing to engine problems – which would later prove to have been grossly exaggerated by *Canopus*' engineering officer – his ship was capable of making only 10kts in the present weather conditions and could in no way be counted on to support the remainder of the squadron. Even at her best possible speed, the ageing battleship could never have reached the battle in time to have any influence on its outcome and thus, in lieu of any request for assistance, Cradock's signal was fated to become another reference point for the enemy's position.

But von Spee, as experienced a mariner as his adversary, appreciated the dangers posed by Cradock's change of course and, aware that his own crews would have the advantage in any night fighting, turned likewise to port – matching Cradock point for point – in an attempt once more to open up the distance between the two lines of ships. In the process, *Scharnhorst* had gradually pulled ahead of the German line, and now slowed down somewhat in order to allow the remaining ships to rejoin her. Slowly and agonizingly the range between them gradually closed, until a little before 1900hrs when, his squadron rejoined by *Dresden* – *Nürnberg* was still, at this time, some distance to the north – and with his heavy 8.2in. batteries now entering their extreme range, von Spee gave instructions for his ships to turn one point starboard to begin closing the range and ordered his gunners to prepare to fire.

Cradock had observed the German change in course, was aware that *Otranto* was noticeably falling behind and ordered a reduction of speed by one knot. He sent another message to the merchantman urging her to do her utmost to maintain speed with her consorts, but Captain Davidson replied that his engines were working at full capacity and he could make no more speed in the rough swell. Eventually, seeing that action was both imminent and inevitable, the merchantman's captain requested confirmation of whether or not his ship should remain in the line. Cradock's reply is not recorded, but as it was clear that his ship had no real combat value, Davidson kept her to the starboard of *Glasgow*, in an attempt partially to shield her from German fire.

Some ten minutes later, with the range at around 12,300 yards, and having by now achieved his object of delaying long enough to have the setting sun silhouette the enemy ships rather than blinding his own gun crews, the German admiral gave the order for his armoured cruisers to prepare for action; in his own words: 'I had manoeuvred so that the sun in the west could not disturb me. The moon in the east was not yet full, but promised good light during the night, and there were rain squalls in various directions.' It

CRADOCK'S GAMBLE, THE BATTLE OF CORONEL, *c.*1940HRS, 1 NOVEMBER 1914 (pp. 50–51)

The exceptionally rough seas **(1)** during the battle of Coronel emphasized the design flaws of Cradock's two armoured cruisers with tragic consequences, as both vessels were obliged to begin the action with their lower casemates **(2)** sealed in order to prevent ships from being flooded. Therefore, as both squadrons began to engage, the deficiencies in the British vessels were magnified by the fact that they were unable to use their full armament against the enemy.

The quality of the German gunnery was soon demonstrated when *Scharnhorst*'s third broadside destroyed *Good Hope*'s forward 9.2in. turret **(3)**, and this effectively meant that Cradock would need to rely upon his secondary 6in. **(4)** armament if he were to engage the enemy effectively.

Here, with his ship ablaze from stem to stern, Cradock is subjected to exceptionally accurate fire by the German heavy guns and is obliged to steer for the enemy cruisers **(5)** in order to close the range and bring his guns to bear.

Even as he makes this last, courageous gesture, the outcome of the battle is no longer – if it ever was – in doubt. With the darkness illuminated by the countless fires blazing **(6)** throughout the stricken ship, either Cradock or – if he has already, by this stage, fallen – Captain Francklin, will continue with his brave advance until the contents of one of her magazines ignites and explodes, the ship disappearing without a trace in the pitch blackness, taking her commander and crew with her, the first of the two British warships to pay the ultimate price.

should be noted, however, that in their reports of the battle *Glasgow's* officers stated that they saw neither the rain showers that von Spee mentions here nor the heavy cloud cover that other German sources have mentioned.

In such conditions, and with his scratch crews having had little opportunity for gunnery practice throughout their crossing of the Atlantic and subsequent journey along the coast of South America, it is doubtful that Cradock's vessel could have accurately fought her forward turret whose 9.2in. gun was one of the only two such weapons in the British squadron that could match the German guns for size and range. Therefore, even as the battle of Coronel began, its outcome was never truly in doubt. At approximately 11,400 yards, the flanks of the German armoured cruisers blossomed with flame, and the first salvo of heavy shells arced towards the enemy line, churning the sea still further as they plunged into the water 500 yards in front of *Good Hope*. Scant seconds later a second salvo thundered into the British flagship's wake and then, almost inevitably, the third salvo crashed into *Good Hope's* bows destroying her forward turret. *Gneisenau's* fire, directed against *Monmouth*, was just as devastatingly effective and, within minutes of the engagement beginning in earnest, the foredecks of both British armoured cruisers had already begun to resemble just so much scrap metal.

With his heaviest ordnance now out of action, Cradock's only real hope was to close the range as quickly as possible and get close enough for his secondary armament to be able effectively to answer the German guns. But even as the two cruisers steamed towards the enemy, each minute that passed simply served to increase their tactical disadvantages. Approaching the German line at a slightly oblique angle, a number of British guns began to reply, firing as soon as they were able to bear upon the approaching ships. *Monmouth*, it should be noted, had commenced her participation in the battle by opening up a brisk fire upon *Gneisenau*, but she was at extreme range for her guns and the damage inflicted on the German cruiser was mainly superficial and was easily repaired; in the main their fire was sporadic and ineffective, and even as the British 6in. guns were able to find their range, so did their opponents' more modern 5.9 and 4.1in. weapons. Then, as the

Captain John Seagrave of AMC *Orama*. Seagrave's vessel supported the final stages of the hunt for *Dresden*.
(IWM, Q069048)

German cruisers' secondary armament began to play a role in the battle, the odds against Cradock and his captains became almost impossibly greater.

In the words of Robert K. Massie, the German return fire resembled that of a peacetime exercise at which both ships' crews excelled, their salvoes thundering out with deadly regularity every 20 seconds. This is not to imply, however, that the German crews did not have to contend with the elements for, as one officer wrote, 'Water foamed up over the cruiser's forecastles and then flowed streaming over the upper decks. The crews and ammunition carriers found it difficult, as a consequence, to maintain their footing.'

Whilst the heavy cruisers engaged their opposite numbers, the German light cruisers now began to take part in the battle with *Dresden* opening fire on *Otranto* which led her to shelter closer in *Glasgow*'s wake, but it was a pair of 8.2in. shells from *Gneisenau* which landed within 50 yards of the liner's bridge that led her captain to pull his ship out of formation and steer for the west in an attempt to escape the enemy fire. The odds, already stacked against the British squadron, had now become almost prohibitive with the initiative quickly slipping out of Cradock's hands.

Until now the action had lasted only a little over 20 minutes and, unable to respond adequately, the leading British ships were being punished remorselessly as shell after shell smashed into their superstructures, often penetrating deep into their hulls and igniting fires that soon ran out of control, their flames serving to illuminate both *Monmouth* and *Good Hope* against the falling darkness.

By this stage, the range had shrunk to 6,000 yards and, as the line continued its seemingly inexorable advance, von Spee – fearing a torpedo attack – again made a turn to the east, but even as he took this evasive action his ships continued with the destruction of the British warships. Targeted as she was by *Gneisenau* – perhaps the finest gunnery ship in the Imperial Navy – *Monmouth*, in particular, suffered grievously, the enemy shells obliterating her forward turret and then literally tearing her bows apart before blasting their way through the lower decks where the resulting fires soon began to rage out of control. Listing heavily to port, the blazing *Monmouth* fell out of formation and it was left to Cradock himself, on the bridge of his stricken flagship, to press home his desperate attack.

Scharnhorst and *Gneisenau*, battle of Coronel. Their finest hour. Designed to be the best of their type, the two German armoured cruisers combine to batter Cradock's squadron.
(Author's collection)

Despite the relative proximity of the opposing ships, in almost total darkness with the moon now partially obscured by clouds, both *Scharnhorst* and *Gneisenau* were almost invisible to the British gunners, their position revealed only by the muzzle flashes that rippled along their broadsides with deadly regularity. Unsure of their exact position, Cradock ordered Captain Philip Francklin to steer directly for what he believed to be the German flagship. Facing him, the German ships suffered no such handicap as their gun layers needed simply to aim for the floating bonfires that were *Good Hope* and *Monmouth*.

Despite the maelstrom of enemy gunfire, and with her upper port-side 6in. battery defiantly answering the German broadsides, *Good Hope* pushed ever onwards, trailing vast columns of smoke and flame, no longer the flagship of a battle squadron but rather the embodiment of her commander and crew's desire to strike one palpable hit on the enemy, a gesture of defiance against the incompetence that had brought them to this position. One cannot know Cradock's thoughts – or indeed those of his men – in these climactic moments of the battle, but in answer to Nelson's exhortation at Trafalgar a century before, whatever fate faced them, they would do their duty.

With the approach of the enemy cruiser fully visible, von Spee waited for a few moments to allow the range to close still further and then ordered both *Scharnhorst* and *Gneisenau* to manoeuvre out of *Good Hope*'s path and as they did so, they began to pour concentrated fire into the British warship. By 1950hrs, the battle had lasted less than an hour and the British flagship lay almost dead in the water, tantalizingly close to her German opposite number. Up to this point she had taken at least 35 direct hits from *Scharnhorst*'s main batteries as well as a significant number from her secondary – 5.9in. – guns and still the shells continued to inexorably hammer into the, by now, defenceless hulk.

Then the darkness was torn apart by a massive explosion which stunned and blinded many observers – at first the crew of *Glasgow*, bringing up the rear of Cradock's line, believed that their commander had achieved a singular but costly victory against his opponent and destroyed the enemy flagship, but as visibility returned to normal they could once again see the German muzzle

Destruction of the British Squadron off the Chilean coast. Similar to many other representations of the battle, this German postcard gives an emotive rendering of the destruction of Cradock's force. (Author's collection)

flashes rippling out. One of her deck officers who had been observing the flagship's progress reported that he had seen 'her funnels illuminated by a fire burning near the bridge. A moment later there was a tremendous detonation… and the whole of her forepart shot up in a fan-shaped sheet of flame.'

Standing on his own bridge, Maximilian von Spee was as close a witness as any of his officers to *Good Hope*'s final moments and in his diary later wrote, 'She looked like a splendid firework display against a dark sky. The glowing white flames mingled with bright green stars, shot up to a great height.'

With the explosion, much of the ship's upper works were hurled into the air and, as they came to land in the swell, *Good Hope*'s bows began to settle, eventually detaching themselves from the main part of the hull which then started to roll and, as it did so, almost in a final gesture of defiance, the port after battery fired twice at her antagonist. As the wreck took on more water, many of the internal fires were extinguished and soon what had once been a funeral pyre was lit only by the dull red glow of heated metal. With the focus of the battle now transferring to the listing *Monmouth*, there were no witnesses to *Good Hope*'s final moments and at around 2000hrs, unnoticed by any of the combatants, she sank beneath the waves.

Some distance to the rear, *Glasgow* now received the attention of *Gneisenau*'s gunners and it became clear to Captain Luce that no purpose would be served by his remaining at the site of Cradock's sacrifice. To stay would simply consign his ship to destruction. At 2005hrs, he gave orders for his ship to cease fire. It was a wise decision and the only realistic one to be made in the circumstances – in less than an hour, the enemy had reduced the two most powerful ships in the squadron to burning wrecks and the best testament to the accuracy and skill of the gunners aboard the German heavy cruisers is to compare them with the achievements of *Dresden* and *Leipzig* who – between them – fired over 600 shells at *Glasgow* and scored only five hits, only one of which was to cause significant damage when it struck the hull near the port outer propeller.

Despite the precariousness of his own position, Luce steered towards the stricken *Monmouth* to see if there was anything that could be done for her. After a hurried exchange with her captain, Frank Brandt, who advised of his ship's extreme situation, it was agreed that Luce could do nothing for the ailing cruiser and, believing that Brandt intended to try to beach his ship on the neutral Chilean shore, he ordered *Glasgow* to steer a course north-west, slowly bringing her up to full speed to quickly outdistance the enemy. As *Glasgow* passed *Monmouth*'s stern, she was greeted by the sight of a number of her crew, silhouetted against the raging fires and waving their arms in salute, their cheers being carried eerily across the water. It was a necessary duty, but nonetheless a deeply disturbing and painful one that left many of *Glasgow*'s crew in a state of shock. One of her officers was later to write 'We were humiliated to the very depths of our beings. We hardly spoke to one another for the first twenty four hours. We felt so bitterly ashamed of ourselves for we had let down the King; we had let down the Admiralty; we had let down England – What would the British people think of the Royal Navy?'

As their ship gradually changed course, finally to come onto the southerly heading which would ultimately take her into *Canopus*' path, observers on *Glasgow* saw a number of searchlight beams flickering across the northern horizon and then came the sound of firing. With bated breath they counted no less than 75 muzzle flashes and then came darkness and an abrupt silence, which could only signal the loss of *Monmouth*.

When it had become clear that both of Cradock's armoured cruisers were *hors de combat*, von Spee signalled his light cruisers to close with the rest of the squadron, 'both British cruisers severely damaged and one light cruiser apparently fairly intact – pursue and attack with torpedoes'.

Despite the moonlight and the illumination from the burning *Monmouth*, the situation remained confused and as *Leipzig* now crossed the area where *Good Hope* had gone down, sailors on her decks threw crates and flotation devices into the water in the hope that some of the bodies that they observed were still alive. No one had the opportunity to report this to their captain as a number of searchlights soon began to arc out of the darkness, signalling the presence of another warship in the vicinity and, as a result, von Spee was to remain ignorant of the loss of the enemy flagship.

Stumbling upon the scene, Captain Lüdecke in *Dresden* believed that he had come across the lone British light cruiser that von Spee had mentioned, immediately ordering his crew to prepare to attack her with torpedoes, and it was only at the last moment that disaster was averted when *Leipzig* was recognized and the attack called off.

Earlier, when von Spee had ordered his squadron to concentrate, *Nürnberg* had been the farthest away from the fighting and unsure of the position of the other vessels, her captain – von Schönberg – simply steered in the direction of the last gunfire that he had observed. At 2040hrs the German light cruiser came upon the heavily damaged *Monmouth* which, despite a list of ten degrees to port, was still gamely trying to make some headway in the heavy seas.

Approaching to within a few hundred yards, *Nürnberg* began slowly to circle the stricken vessel and, as her searchlights played upon the shattered superstructure, one of the deck officers called upon the British warship to strike her colours – to which there was no reply, the White Ensign fluttering defiantly above the burning cruiser. At 2050hrs, von Schönberg gave the order for a warning shot to be fired as an incentive for the British captain to lower the flag, but the only perceived movement on the *Monmouth* was that of the damage repair parties, endeavouring against all the odds to keep her afloat. Satisfied that he had sufficiently followed the Rules of War and that *Monmouth* was still a combatant vessel, von Schönberg ordered a torpedo attack to be carried out, but the weapon missed and so he called for the searchlights to be switched off whilst he waited for the enemy's next move. The scene was fully illuminated by the fires raging unchecked on the British cruiser.

Suddenly, *Monmouth* began to gather speed and turn towards her adversary. Fearing an attack, von Schönberg ordered his ship to come about on *Monmouth*'s stern, and as she did so *Nürnberg* opened fire with a devastating broadside at point-blank range. The German gunners couldn't fail to hit their target, the shells tearing into the already stricken ship, which began to heel ever farther to port and slowly capsized a little after 2100hrs, her proud ensigns remaining defiant to the last.

Even as the British warship sank beneath the waves, the alarm bells rang out on *Nürnberg*'s decks as her lookouts spotted at least one unidentified four-funnelled ship closing on their position and von Schönberg immediately gave orders for evasive action to be taken. In his after-action report, he would cite – understandably – the heavy seas, the fact that his own lifeboats were fully secured for combat, and the possible presence of at least one enemy heavy cruiser as the grounds for his failure to make any attempt to search for enemy survivors. The ships turned out to be *Scharnhorst* and *Gneisenau*,

IN THE FINEST TRADITION OF THE SERVICE, THE BATTLE OF CORONEL, *c.*2050HRS, 1 NOVEMBER 1914 (pp. 58–59)

Like her consort, *Good Hope*, HMS *Monmouth* was virtually obsolete in comparison with the smaller, but better-protected and heavier-armed cruisers that formed the core of the East Asia Squadron. With *Scharnhorst* engaging the British flagship, it fell to *Gneisenau* to engage her opposite number in the enemy line, and the unequal combat soon saw the British cruiser crippled (**1**) before her opponent turned her attentions to *Good Hope*.

Shattered by gunfire, *Monmouth* which, at this stage in the battle, is already ablaze both above and below decks (**2**), and listing heavily to port (**3**), is also settling down by the bows (**4**), which had already been ripped apart by enemy gunfire.

Believing the *Monmouth*'s captain, Frank Brandt, intends to beach his ship and unable to influence the battle, Captain John Luce orders *Glasgow* to steer for open water, and about 20 minutes later, the German light cruiser, *Nürnberg* (**5**), comes upon the stricken vessel.

Circling the enemy ship, and illuminating her with searchlights, *Nürnberg* calls upon *Monmouth* to surrender (**6**) and strike her colours. The sole response was for the work parties on *Monmouth*'s decks to attempt to bring her rear turret into action (**7**), and for the ship herself to reverse engines and head towards the German vessel.

Fearing a torpedo attack, von Schönberg – the German captain – orders all lights extinguished and pulls away, opening up the range between the two ships. In a one-sided engagement, *Nürnberg* then begins to bombard the British cruiser at point-blank range and at a little before 2100hrs *Monmouth* will sink with all hands, the German captain later stating that the rough seas had prevented him from making an attempt to rescue any survivors.

but it was now too late for the German captain to correct his mistake, and however unpalatable it may have been for them many of his officers would endorse his position that the Rules of War had been observed.

As Leutnant Otto von Spee, the admiral's son was to write in his diary, 'It was terrible to have to fire on poor fellows who were unable to defend themselves, but their colours were still flying and when we ceased fire for several minutes they did not haul them down.'

In the increasing darkness, von Spee took stock of his situation. *Monmouth* had been confirmed as sunk whilst, to the best of his knowledge, *Good Hope* had limped away so badly damaged that she would either sink overnight or – if lucky – would make the Chilean coast. He would endeavour to persuade the government there to intern her for the duration of hostilities. The status and position of both *Glasgow* and *Otranto* were immaterial to him, the former being too small to pose a threat whilst the latter was too slow and unwieldy to cause him concern.

The following morning, von Spee gave orders for the light cruisers to conduct a thorough search for *Good Hope*, and it was now that he received Haun's belated report of the fate of the British flagship. It was clear that, with the sinking of the two British armoured cruisers, he had command of the seas and the fact that *Scharnhorst* had taken only two superficial hits and her consort, *Gneisenau*, only four seemed to reinforce this. However, the German admiral was more than aware that in this single action his heavy ships had between them expended a significant proportion of their primary 8.2in. ammunition (*Scharnhorst* had only 350 shells remaining, *Gneisenau* 528) and the only source of resupply for them was either of the main naval bases in Germany itself, Kiel or Wilhelmshaven. In short, by virtue of its victory, the Ostasiengeschwader had compromised its capacity for future combat.

In a private assessment of his situation, von Spee was torn between the obvious euphoria of victory and a rational acknowledgement that, had luck not been on his side, things could have been very different:

> *Good Hope*, though bigger than *Scharnhorst*, was not so well armed. She mounted heavy guns, but only two, while *Monmouth* succumbed to *Gneisenau* because she had only 6in guns. The British have another ship like *Monmouth* hereabouts and in addition, it seems, a battleship of the Queen class carrying 12in guns. Against the latter we can hardly do anything. Had they kept their force together, we would probably have got the worst of it.

On 3 November, the bulk of the squadron sailed into Valparaiso to an enthusiastic welcome, both by the local German community and the crews of a number of German merchantmen who had been driven into port to seek protection from *Glasgow* and *Monmouth*. At a reception at the city's German Club, when one of the guests boorishly proposed the toast 'Damnation to the Royal Navy!' Admiral von Spee declared that neither he nor his men would make such a gesture. Instead, he raised his glass, 'To the memory of a brave and gallant enemy' and thereafter returned to his flagship.

Taking the time to meet an old naval comrade who lived in the city, von Spee confided that he had no doubts about the final outcome of his voyage: 'I cannot reach Germany; we possess no secure harbour; I must plough the seas of the world, doing as much damage to the enemy before my ammunition is expended or a superior foe catches up with me and brings me to battle.' His words would prove to be disturbingly prescient.

HMS *Invincible*. The first of Fisher's greyhounds, *Invincible* would narrowly escape destruction at the Falklands, only to meet the same fate at Jutland two years later. (Author's collection)

A COSTLY DELAY

After leaving Valaparaiso, von Spee sailed once again to Más Afuera where the squadron refuelled with American coal that had been purchased previously by *Leipzig*. Inexplicably he then chose to remain on the island for nine days. He knew that Britain would be organizing her response to the defeat at Coronel and a commander with his reputation for decisiveness should have been rushing southwards in order to clear Cape Horn and the Magellan Straits as quickly as possible. However, he allowed his crews to rest. Many commentators have offered their own explanations for this apparent lethargy, ranging from fatalism in the face of the incalculable odds ranged against his squadron to anxiety over the depleted state of his ammunition bunkers. Any of these could in some way have been a contributory factor, but in the final analysis it was simply in his interest to enter the South Atlantic at the earliest possible juncture in order to pull any pursuing forces away from their own coaling stations. Simply put, any force coming southwards to bar his entry into the South Atlantic would have exhausted its own coal stocks and would need to take on fuel at the Falklands which would obviously take time, time which would allow the German admiral to slip farther away into international waters with the continued possibility of taking on further supplies of fuel from friendly or neutral merchantmen.

Raising anchor on 15 November, the Ostasiengeschwader followed the Chilean coastline southwards, reaching the Bahía San Quintin four days later where von Spee halted once again to reconsider his options. It was here that he received a signal from Berlin to the effect that, in recognition of his victory, the Kaiser had awarded him the Iron Cross 1st and 2nd Class and that – at his discretion – a further 300 men of the squadron were to receive the 2nd Class award.

Whilst at San Quintin, von Spee received a second communiqué in which the fragmented organization of the Imperial Navy once again showed itself as von Tirpitz made the overt suggestion that the Ostasiengeschwader should capitalize on the success of Coronel by striking into the Atlantic and making a dash for Germany which would be ultimately supported by a sortie of the High Seas Fleet which would 'bring the victorious warriors home'. Von Tirpitz, however, was not the operational head of the navy and his suggestions were precisely that. Von Pohl, who held the command, was made of more cautious stuff and simply advised that von Spee should act on his own initiative. Thus given carte blanche, the admiral elected for the only realistic option and, encouraged by the promised resupply of 40,000 tons of American coal, advised his superiors that he would make the attempt to evade any pursuit and reach home.

Raising anchor on 26 November, the squadron sailed southwards towards the Magellan Straits, encountering increasingly heavy seas in which even von Spee's heavy cruisers found themselves in difficulty. On the 29th conditions had deteriorated to such a degree that all ships draped themselves with emergency rope lines to which crewmen could attach themselves whilst performing essential duties. The light cruisers, naturally, had it much worse than their heavier sisters and deck cargoes were cast overboard to preserve trim. As one officer later wrote: 'The seas were huge, at one minute level with the deck, next forty feet below you.... We sheered out of line as heavy seas shifted the deck cargo and with the scuppers blocked with coal we took three feet of water on deck and were really in danger of capsizing.... We turned into the wind and all hands turned out in order to shovel the loose coal overboard, all this whilst standing waist deep in icy water.'

Eventually the high winds calmed somewhat, but the German ships still had to deal with the heavy rain and hailstorms that alternately battered their superstructures. Rounding Cape Horn on 1 December, the crews' morale was lifted slightly by the capture of a British three-master carrying almost 3,000 tons of prime Welsh coal. Anchoring in the shelter of Picton Island on the southern tip of Tierra del Fuego, the Ostasiengeschwader remained for three days whilst supplies of coal were redistributed and the men recovered from their recent ordeal. As the men rested, von Spee called his captains together on the morning of 6 December to discuss what, to all intents and purposes, was the beginning of the final stage of their journey home.

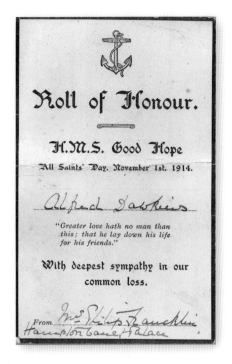

'In Memoriam'. Roll of honour for the crew of *Good Hope*, established by the widow of her commander, Captain Philip Francklin RN. (Coronel Memorial)

A rare photograph showing von Spee's squadron rounding Cape Horn in abysmal weather conditions, 1 December 1914. (IWM, Q05992)

In the spartan interior of *Scharnhorst*'s wardroom, von Spee proposed that the squadron launch a surprise attack upon the Falkland Islands before disappearing into the South Atlantic and making its way back home. The subsequent fate of the Ostasiengeschwader means that we have no concrete evidence regarding the rationale behind von Spee's decision to make this last attack and modern commentators have variously ascribed it to hubris, fatigue caused by the strain of having to evade Allied attempts at pursuit, the location of a wireless station and coaling facilities, or the intention of capturing the Islands' British governor as an act of retaliation for the enemy capture of the German governors of Samoa and German New Guinea. We can therefore only speculate about any personal reasons behind the admiral's motives for the attack, but militarily there is one variable which is fully borne out by subsequent events; any British or Allied force operating in the South Atlantic – in pursuit of von Spee – would be operating at the extreme edge of its effective range and, without the possibility of adequate refuelling on the Falkland Islands, it would be forced to withdraw northwards to one of the other coaling stations, all of which would take precious time, time during which the German squadron would draw increasingly farther away from any pursuit.

Of those present, only one of the squadron's captains – von Schönberg of *Nürnberg* – chose to voice his support for the plan, whilst many of the others kept their reservations to themselves. Gustav Märker, the captain of *Gneisenau* and a long-time friend of the admiral was particularly vociferous in his opposition, viewing it as an unnecessary diversion. However, rank and responsibility travel hand in hand so von Spee had the final word on the subject. He decided that only a detachment of the squadron would make the actual attack whilst the remainder waited in support out of sight of land, and instructed his most trusted subordinate to draft an operational plan.

Despite his personal misgivings, Märker's plan was conscientiously prepared and, given the intelligence available to von Spee, had every chance of success; once the squadron came within reach of the Falkland Islands,

HMS *Inflexible*. Sister ship to *Invincible*, Fisher's decision to send a second battle cruiser to the South Atlantic proved crucial to the successful outcome to the campaign. (IWM, Q039267)

Gneisenau and *Nürnberg* (obviously von Schönberg's reward for endorsing an attack) would be detached from the squadron and then sail to a point some five miles east of the Cape Pembroke lighthouse, a location from which they could observe the anchorage around Stanley. If the area were clear of enemy warships, *Gneisenau* would then proceed to the harbour entrance and launch boats to clear any mines. Once this was completed, *Nürnberg* would sail into the inner harbour and cover the landing parties sent ashore to destroy the wireless station and coaling facilities. When all this had been achieved, they would put to sea again and rejoin the squadron. In his estimates, Märker believed that if he had passed the lighthouse by 0830hrs, he would be back with the formation no later than 1930hrs. The plan was endorsed by von Spee and, on the morning of 7 December, the squadron put to sea, its bows pointing towards the Falkland Islands.

THE BATTLE OF THE FALKLAND ISLANDS

On 2 November, and with no way of contacting Cradock directly, the British consul in Valparaiso sent an urgent telegram to the Admiralty in London, advising of von Spee's arrival and requesting that the information be urgently relayed to the local naval commander. Tragically, he had no way of knowing that the two squadrons had met on the previous afternoon and that the Royal Navy had suffered its first defeat in almost a century.

Battenberg had been hounded out of office on account of a perceived loyalty to Germany, the land of his birth, and the new First Sea Lord, 'Jacky' Fisher sent an immediate dispatch to Cradock ordering him under no circumstances to seek battle with von Spee, but instead to remain concentrated on *Canopus* with *Glasgow* detached for scouting purposes until such time as he received adequate reinforcement. The fickleness of fate being such that *Defence*, then at Montevideo, was finally ordered to join his command 'with the utmost dispatch'. Had Cradock's original orders been less ambiguous, then *Defence* might still have found him at Stanley on the Falkland Islands, but Coronel and Valparaiso were over two weeks' sailing from the Uruguayan capital and any contest off the Chilean coast would have been resolved long before her arrival.

Before long, the first reports of the defeat began to arrive from German sources, but were consistently denied by the Admiralty for the simple reason that *Canopus* was never mentioned in any of these reports and – as was made clear – the elderly battleship was an integral part of Cradock's squadron. Therefore, if *Canopus* were not involved, then it could only be a question of German misinformation. By 6 November, the official line had changed somewhat, when the Admiralty admitted that an action had been fought and that it had been 'most gallantly contested, but in the absence of *Canopus*, the enemy's preponderance of force was considerable'. In short, the official line was that the presence of an obsolete warship that had only recently been reprieved from the scrapyard would have staved off disaster at the hands of a crack German squadron.

At home, opinion was divided. Many questioned Cradock's rationale for seeking battle against a demonstrably superior enemy but just as many questioned the superiors who had placed him in such a position with inadequate resources and then repeatedly failed to act upon the recommendations of 'the man on the spot'. Cradock's cause was also taken up by David Beatty, who eulogized his old friend and comrade in arms and who had no doubt about

Movements before the battle of the Falkland Islands

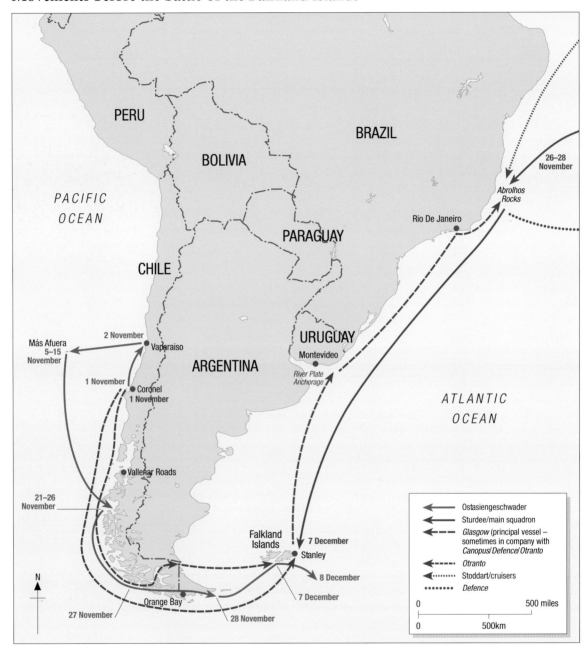

where the blame for the disaster lay: 'He had a glorious death, but if only it had been in victory instead of defeat…. His death, the loss of his ships and the lives of the gallant men can be laid at the door of the incompetency of the Admiralty. They have time and time again broken every rule of strategy.'

With the defeat at Coronel now freely and openly admitted, the task that faced the Admiralty was how finally to bring von Spee to battle and resolve the threat he posed. The first reaction was immediately to reinforce Stoddart's squadron, which was now to be based off Montevideo, and both *Glasgow* and *Otranto* were ordered to sail there whilst the slow-moving *Canopus* was beached at Stanley to protect the harbour. With *Defence*

already en situ, the final addition was armoured cruiser *Kent* which had been ordered to join Stoddart from Sierra Leone. In London, Churchill proposed to make any future combat academic by detaching a battle cruiser from the Grand Fleet, but Fisher went further and overruled his colleague by ordering both *Invincible* and her sister ship *Inflexible* to make for the South Atlantic, whilst a third battle cruiser, *Princess Royal*, was to make way to Central America and cover the northern entrance to the Panama Canal. His purpose was 'not merely to defeat von Spee but rather to annihilate him'. For the First Sea Lord this would be the acid test of the rationale behind the battle cruisers' *raison d'être*. Although he apologized in the face of vehement protestation from the commander of the Grand Fleet, Sir John Jellicoe, and the commander of the Battle Cruiser Squadron, Sir David Beatty, Fisher stuck to his guns, all the while insisting that all of von Spee's options needed to be considered and countered.

Having successfully overruled the senior officers concerned, Fisher now found himself embroiled in yet another argument, this time with Churchill. The problem arose from the fact that the addition of the battle cruisers to the task force warranted the appointment of a vice admiral as commander and there were few officers of this rank available for service at short notice and, as a result, Churchill's choice fell upon Sir Frederick Sturdee, the Naval Chief of Staff. The problem was that Sturdee had, years earlier, sided against Fisher in a dispute with a fellow admiral and, ever since, Fisher had blamed him for every misfortune to befall the navy since the outbreak of war, stating that his methods of deployment were designed to make the Royal Navy 'weak everywhere and strong nowhere' and that the man himself was 'a pedantic ass: is, was and always will be.'

On 5 November 1914, the two battle cruisers left their station in the Cromarty Firth and four days later made landfall at the naval base at Devonport, near Plymouth, where they were both to undergo emergency repairs. The urgency of the situation was lost on the Commander in Chief (Plymouth), Admiral Sir George Egerton, who advised the Admiralty that neither ship would be in a position to sail before 13 November. For the two First Lords this was patently unacceptable and at Fisher's they urging fired off a communiqué that was designed to leave Egerton in no doubt about his options:

Princess Royal. The third battle cruiser detached from the Grand Fleet was sent to block the northern entrance to the Panama Canal. (IWM, SP001683)

> *Invincible* and *Inflexible* are needed for War Service and are to sail Wednesday 11 November. Dockyard arrangements must be made to conform. You are responsible for the speedy dispatch of these ships in a thoroughly efficient condition. If necessary, dockyard men should be sent away in the ships, to return as opportunity offers.

The ships fully laden, and running repairs still under way, the two battle cruisers left port as prescribed, at noon on 11 November, their first port of call being Saint Vincent in the Cape Verde Islands, off the coast of Africa, some 2,500 miles distant. From Saint Vincent they would cross the Atlantic to link up with Stoddart at the Abrolhos Rocks, a journey of almost the same length, where Sturdee was to receive the latest intelligence about von Spee's whereabouts as well as fresh instructions from the Admiralty. These were indeed waiting for him as he was immediately instructed to, 'Proceed south with colliers and whole squadron. Use Falkland Islands as main base for colliers and after coaling proceed to Chilean coast, avoid letting your large ships be seen in the Magellan Straits. Search the straits, inlets and channels taking colliers with you as necessary.'

With a force now comprising his two battle cruisers to which were added Stoddart's five ships (*Carnarvon*, *Cornwall*, *Glasgow*, *Bristol* and the armed liner *Orama*) as well as the newly arrived *Kent* and another armed liner, *Macedonia*, it was believed that Sturdee had more than sufficient firepower and tactical flexibility to accomplish his task of 'annihilating' von Spee and his squadron. On the morning of 28 November, Sturdee – under pressure from John Luce of *Glasgow* – ordered his reinforced command to put to sea and his ships began the final leg of their 7,500 mile journey to the southern edge of the world.

With the ships deployed in an extended line to trap a German liner – the *Kronprinz Wilhelm*, which had been reported operating off the River Plate – the squadron continued southwards at a relatively gentle speed of 11kts, a tacit acknowledgement that, the coaling facilities on the Falklands notwithstanding, the ships would be operating at the extreme limit of their range and any setback, whether mechanical or fuel related could have disastrous consequences. The nearest dockyard facility that could resupply or repair either of the capital ships was probably Gibraltar, some 5,000 miles away and thus for Sturdee, as ultimately for his German counterpart, failure was simply not an option.

Two days out to sea, and recognizing the German armoured cruisers' reputation as crack gunnery ships, Sturdee ordered that the two battle cruisers should carry out some gunnery practice, the range to be 12,000 yards which was the distance at which he had already decided was the optimum to engage the enemy squadron. First up was *Invincible,* which was to fire four rounds from each of her main guns at a target towed by *Inflexible* before returning the compliment. The results were ominous to say the least with the flagship succeeding with a single hit out of 32 shells, whilst her sister scored marginally better with three hits – some degree of success was derived however by the apparent number of 'near misses' achieved by both ships and the mantra that 'a German cruiser is significantly larger than a towed marker'. The practice almost ended in disaster, however, when *Invincible* began to reel in her target and the towing cable became fouled on one of her outer propellers, forcing her to complete the rest of her journey under reduced power.

With the squadron continuing deeper into the southern latitudes, the weather began steadily to worsen and this change was finally recognized on

S. M. Panzerkreuzer Gneisenau

SMS *Gneisenau*. 'The Best of the Best', perhaps the crack gunnery ship of the Imperial German Navy, *Gneisenau* was a key element of the Ostasiengeschwader.

4 December when the crews were ordered to change their 'summer whites' for 'winter blues'. Three days later, after a total voyage of 27 days, at 1026hrs on Monday 7 December, *Invincible* dropped anchor in Port William, the deep water anchorage which served the coaling station at Stanley on East Falkland. Almost immediately, divers were sent down into the calm waters of the bay in order to clear *Invincible*'s fouled propeller whilst the remainder of the squadron prepared to take on fresh supplies of coal and individual ships commenced work on any minor repairs necessary after the long journey.

That evening, Sturdee summoned his captains aboard the flagship and shared the latest intelligence reports that had been waiting for him at Government House; German colliers had been reported as having been sighted both in the estuary of the River Plate, off Montevideo, and off Dawson Island in the centre of the Magellan Straits. The concentration of these support vessels and their locations were a sure sign that von Spee had not – as yet – made any move into the South Atlantic and, anticipating an extensive search, Sturdee gave instructions that all ships should not only continue to fill their bunkers but also, in order to increase their range, provision should be made for the storage of bagged coal on decks and in walkways. Detailed orders would then be drafted and sent to each ship, the squadron itself was to sail for Cape Horn on the evening of 8 December which was when, it was anticipated, the battle cruisers would themselves have completed their coaling.

At 0530hrs on the morning of Tuesday 8 December, the crew of *Invincible* was called on deck to begin the long and arduous task of coaling, a process which would see almost 200 tons loaded into the bunkers every hour and thus, punctuated by mealtimes, would continue into the early evening. Unbeknown to the sweating sailors, the task would not be completed that day for, at the same time, the enemy force that they had been sent to find and destroy was perilously close and Märker's detachment already under way to its objective.

Unlike the adverse conditions that had continually battered both squadrons on the way to the South Atlantic, the weather on this fateful morning was almost perfect. The sea was calm, being gently rippled by a breeze from the north-west, whilst the skies above were clear and blue and under the aegis of bright sunshine the two German warships headed eastwards, each minute bringing them ever closer to the unsuspecting British settlement.

The first sign that something was amiss came when the two ships drew abreast of the lighthouse when observers saw what they believed to be a thin column of smoke rising into the air, a phenomenon that could only indicate the presence of a ship.

Ashore, and at roughly the same time a civilian lookout on the high ground west of Stanley saw two columns of smoke to the south-west and called in the sighting to Captain Grant on the beached *Canopus*. With no direct communication to Sturdee's flagship there seemed to be no way that Grant could get the message through to his superior officer short of sending a runner, but then, he spotted *Glasgow* some distance away but closer to Sturdee's position and in the hope that Luce – her captain – would know what to do, hoisted the signal: 'Enemy in Sight'. Luce did indeed act as Grant had hoped and had mirrored the signal on his own yards but, fully engaged in the process of coaling, there seemed to be no reaction on *Invincible* until Luce ordered a gun to be fired and had a searchlight trained on the flagship's bridge before the vital message was finally received.

Had he but known, von Spee had achieved complete surprise with the British squadron fatally dispersed between the two anchorages with only *Carnarvon* and *Glasgow* having completed their coaling and none of the ships, with the exception of the piquet ship – *Kent* – ready for sea and in a position to fight. Of the remainder, both *Bristol* and *Cornwall* were ruled out of any impending engagement, each ship having stripped down at least one engine for repairs. A bold stroke by the German admiral would have subjected the confines of the harbour to a storm of fire from both his primary and secondary armament which would have most certainly wreaked havoc amongst the British vessels as they raised steam and tried to make their way to sea. Coupled with the destructive power and confusion caused by successive waves of torpedoes fired blind into the anchorage, it was simply a disaster waiting to happen, but if luck had been against Cradock at Coronel, it was most certainly with Sturdee on this particular morning.

Aboard his flagship, Sturdee was the epitome of British phlegm when faced with adversity. When he received *Glasgow*'s signal he was in the act of shaving and apparently paused only long enough to order the crew to be sent to breakfast before returning to the task in hand. Soon however, signal flags began to flutter from *Invincible*'s halyards as the squadron commander made his dispositions; *Kent* was to clear the harbour and take up a position to cover the armed liner *Macedonia* that held the position as the outermost sentinel; both battle cruisers were to cease coaling and cast off the colliers in order to be able to clear for action; the armoured cruiser *Carnarvon* was to work up to full steam as quickly as possible and join *Kent* in

Whilst writing a report during the stern chase with *Nürnberg*, Commander Arthur Bedford left his cabin, which took a direct hit during his absence. His uniform coat shows the effects of the German shell. (IWM, UNI012473)

order to be in a position to attack the enemy ships should they round Cape Pembroke; *Canopus* was instructed to open fire once a suitable target presented itself, whilst all other ships were given orders to build up steam and advise the flagship when they were capable of making at least 12kts. It was 0815hrs, a scant 30 minutes after the two German warships had first been sighted.

As the minutes ticked by the observer who had first spotted *Gneisenau* and *Nürnberg* now reported seeing further columns of smoke out to sea, and these were soon confirmed by *Canopus'* gunnery officer who reported that the first enemy group was a little over 8 miles distant whilst the second group was – at that point – roughly 20 miles out to sea.

Within the anchorage all was confusion – supply vessels were being cast off and quickly making their way towards the shore in order to give the warships more room to manoeuvre whilst the steel-hulled behemoths made themselves ready for sea. It would take at least an hour for the majority of the squadron to be in a position to act upon Sturdee's next orders an equation in which *Bristol* and *Cornwall* could not be included as they had to replace their dismantled engines before making any preparations for combat.

Ashore, the Governor of the Falkland Islands sent an immediate signal to the Admiralty which understandably caused severe consternation in the British High Command as it seemingly served to reinforce Fisher's condemnation of Sturdee: 'Admiral Spee arrived at daylight this morning with all his ships and is now in action with Admiral Sturdee's whole fleet which was coaling.'

It seemed as if the German admiral had once again beaten the odds to strike a decisive blow against the Royal Navy and, turning to Sir Henry Oliver, Sturdee's replacement as Naval Chief of Staff, Churchill asked him if – in his opinion – the message meant that Sturdee had been caught and attacked whilst still at anchor. 'I hope not' was the only answer that Oliver could muster.

Aboard the two German cruisers, preparations were now being made for their arrival off Stanley with ships' boats being uncovered and a number of landing parties assembling on *Gneisenau*'s decks. From her upper works numerous pairs of binoculars were now trained on the approaching coastline, their owners continually informing their captain of each new sighting and slowly Märker's appreciation of his position began to change:

> As we approached, signs of life began to appear. Here and there behind the dunes, columns of dark yellow smoke began to ascend... as if stores were being burned to prevent them from falling into our hands.... In any case, we had been seen, for amongst the mastheads which could be made out through the smoke, two (*Carnarvon* and *Kent*) now broke away and began slowly to make their way eastwards towards the lighthouse.... There was no further doubt in my mind that warships lay concealed behind the land.... At first we thought that we could make out two vessels, then four and then six.... We forwarded this information to the Admiral aboard *Scharnhorst*.

Although it was now clear that the enemy had won the race to the Falklands, Märker passed on his intelligence to his superior officer and continued with his mission. When his gunnery officer, Korvettenkapitän Johann Busche, reported seeing tripod masts, the distinguishing feature of British capital ships, Märker chose to ignore his subordinate's report and failed to forward the information to von Spee. The Ostasiengeschwader had emerged virtually

A 4.1in. shell fired from *Leipzig* and recovered from *Cornwall* after the battle of the Falklands. (IWM, MUN003274)

Invincible and Inflexible, photograph taken from Kent. In pursuit – the battle cruisers steaming after Scharnhorst and Gneisenau. (IWM, Q045912)

unscathed from Coronel and, facing almost certain combat, there was every reason to believe that it would do so again if it could reconcentrate before being committed.

With the distance to their objective steadily decreasing, the German captains were unaware that they were being tracked by *Canopus*' guns and at 0920hrs, as the two cruisers rounded Wolf's Rock in order to engage the wireless station, the ageing battleship's forward turret belched flame. At a range of around 11,000 yards the two 12in. shells raced towards their target, ultimately falling short. It was enough. Turning sharply to the south-east the raiders raised their battle ensigns and prepared for action, followed by another two shells from *Canopus*. The elderly warship might have been considered too much of a liability in an engagement at sea, but her participation in the opening phase of the battle of the Falkland Islands had diverted the enemy from his course and had almost certainly given Sturdee the warning and time necessary to get his ships to sea.

After radioing the flagship with the news that he had come under heavy-calibre fire, Märker decided that he could not withdraw without striking a blow at the enemy and ordered his detachment to make for the lone enemy light cruiser (*Kent*) that seemed to be fleeing from Stanley. If he could sink her, then honour would be satisfied. It was not to be. As soon as he had digested the latest information, von Spee signalled *Gneisenau*, ordering her to withdraw and rejoin the remainder of the squadron: 'Do not accept action.... Concentrate on course east by south.... Proceed at full speed.' Although the situation was seemingly spiralling out of control, von Spee was certain that even if the British ships now known to be at Stanley did carry heavy ordnance, they would be only elderly battleships, rusting hulks that his modern cruisers could outrun with ease.

By 0945hrs, *Glasgow* had joined *Kent* outside the harbour entrance, thus providing an outer screen behind which the rest of the squadron could finish their preparations for battle, and slowly they too made their way out to sea. First in line came *Carnarvon*, flying Stoddart's command pennant, and then *Inflexible* followed in succession by *Invincible* – with Sturdee aboard – and *Cornwall*, whose artificers had performed a minor miracle in reassembling her engine and then getting up sufficient steam for her to take part in the action. Behind lay Clinton-Baker's *Bristol,* which was still reassembling her engines, and the auxiliary *Macedonia,* which – the bitter experience of Coronel had shown – had no true place in a naval battle.

With the emergence of the British ships into open water, the advantage seemed to have shifted firmly in Sturdee's favour, with his six warships – as opposed to von Spee's five – giving him a significant numerical and qualitative edge over the German squadron, in addition to which the calm seas and clear skies almost seemed to set the seal on an inevitable British victory. It was, however, to be neither that simple nor that inevitable.

As the Royal Navy squadron slowly worked up to battle speed, each ship flying a white ensign bravely from every mast, Fisher's greyhounds gradually overtook the outlying cruisers. First *Carnarvon* disappeared in their wake and then *Kent* until only *Glasgow* lay before the two battle cruisers, speeding towards their prey some 15 miles distant.

Sturdee's plan was to push his ships in order to bring his main armament into effective range as quickly as possible and then pound the enemy with his 12in. guns from a distance at which their own heavy batteries would be ineffective. With the weather showing no sign of deteriorating it should have been, theoretically, a straightforward matter to overhaul the enemy and then batter him into submission. By his own calculations the battle cruisers would reach optimum range shortly after 1300hrs, which would give him a further six hours – in perfect weather conditions – to accomplish the task. Satisfied that all was as it should be, Sturdee gave instructions that the signal 'General Chase' be hoisted; he had previously instructed his cruiser commanders that the ships would conform to formation while it remained a squadron engagement but if the enemy tried to scatter, each officer was to use his own initiative in pursuing the fleeing enemy and bringing him to battle.

As the line of British ships began to shake itself out, it soon became clear to Märker and his officers that ignoring Busche's report had been a critical error for as Korvettenkapitän Hans Pochhammer, *Gneisenau*'s first officer, was later to write:

> Two vessels soon detached themselves from our pursuers; they seemed much faster and bigger than the other enemy ships as their smoke was thicker, wider, more massive... the possibility, the probability that we were being pursued by British battle cruisers was a bitter pill to swallow... for it meant a life-or-death struggle or, more likely, a battle ending in an honourable death.

Closing with the enemy, but realizing that his armoured cruisers were falling behind, Sturdee began to adjust his dispositions, giving instructions for both *Invincible* and *Inflexible* to reduce speed to 20kts with the latter taking station on the flagship's starboard quarter. *Glasgow* was likewise ordered to slow down whilst *Carnarvon* and *Cornwall* were told to close with the flagship at their best possible speed. Then, at a little after 1130hrs, Sturdee gave instructions that the ships' crews could be sent below decks for their next meal.

Aboard the ships of the Ostasiengeschwader and with action imminent the crews were also given leave to eat their midday meal, but it was overshadowed by a sense of fatality, the feeling that – come what may – many of those present would not survive the next few hours.

Slowly the distance between the two lines of ships closed and Sturdee, seeing that *Carnarvon* was lagging behind – she could make no more than 18kts – ordered her to be left behind and the remaining ships to work up to

The battle of the Falkland Islands

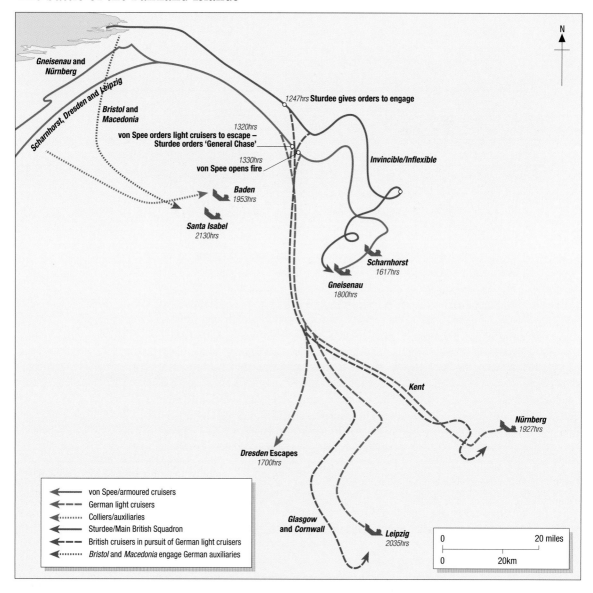

Gneisenau and Nürnberg

Scharnhorst, Dresden and Leipzig

Bristol and Macedonia

1247hrs **Sturdee gives orders to engage**

1320hrs
**von Spee orders light cruisers to escape –
Sturdee orders 'General Chase'**

1330hrs
von Spee opens fire

Invincible/Inflexible

Baden
1953hrs

Santa Isabel
2130hrs

Scharnhorst
1617hrs

Gneisenau
1800hrs

Kent

Nürnberg
1927hrs

Dresden Escapes
1700hrs

Glasgow
and Cornwall

Leipzig
2035hrs

	von Spee/armoured cruisers
	German light cruisers
	Colliers/auxiliaries
	Sturdee/Main British Squadron
	British cruisers in pursuit of German light cruisers
	Bristol and *Macedonia* engage German auxiliaries

0   20 miles

0   20km

their maximum speed. To their front, the enemy formation was led by Märker's detachment some 2,000 yards in front of *Scharnhorst* who had the light cruiser *Dresden* on her port quarter and *Leipzig* some distance astern. In response to Sturdee's increase in speed, von Spee gave similar orders to his own captains and for a few moments the range increased once more and then settled as his rearmost ship began to lag behind.

At 1247hrs, Sturdee hoisted the signal 'Engage the enemy' and eight minutes later *Inflexible* opened fire with her forward turret, sending two 12in. shells arcing towards *Leipzig* at a range of 16,500 yards. The shells fell considerably short, but a few minutes later *Invincible* began her participation in the battle with a salvo that landed a mere thousand yards short of their target and soon the battle cruisers' gunnery officers, Hubert Dannreuther and Rudolf Verner were calling out near misses as the German light cruiser was straddled by towering waterspouts.

On the bridge of the German flagship, von Spee was now confronted by a stark choice; he could either continue to refuse battle in the hope that the majority of his ships could still outdistance the enemy until night fell and gave him a chance to escape in the confusion of darkness, a choice that would force him to sacrifice *Leipzig*, or he could accept the inevitability of combat and accept Sturdee's challenge in the hope that a lucky hit could ensure his squadron's survival. For an officer of von Spee's character and social class, there was only one option available to him and at approximately 1320hrs he signalled his captains that '*Scharnhorst* and *Gneisenau* will accept action. Light cruisers are to part company and try to escape' and with that the *Scharnhorst*, followed by her consort, began to describe an arc east by northeast, placing themselves directly in the path of the oncoming battle cruisers, even as the three light cruisers turned starboard, making for the south-west.

It was the moment that John Luce in *Glasgow* had been waiting for, ever since he had suffered the ignominy of having to leave *Monmouth* to her fate at Coronel and as soon as the German light cruisers began their turn, he swung out of position in front of *Inflexible* and, with *Cornwall* and *Kent* following in his wake, began to give chase.

The action that now unfolded was almost a reverse image of Coronel. The German admiral was now driving his ships across an almost glasslike ocean in an attempt to close the range sufficiently for his main armament to have a chance of penetrating the enemy armour, whilst his erstwhile foe was more than ready to keep the range open long enough for superior firepower to decide the issue; even as von Spee made his move, the British battle cruisers were turning farther to port in order to maintain the advantage conferred by their heavier guns.

By 1330hrs von Spee was on a parallel heading to the enemy and gave the order to open fire. Although – as expected – the rounds fell short, the second salvo inched closer to its target quickly followed by a third broadside that straddled *Invincible*. Aboard the British flagship, one of her officers remarked admiringly upon the German firing, noting that it was 'magnificent to watch, with perfect salvoes rippling along their sides. A brown coloured puff with a centre of flame marking each gun as it fired.... They straddled us time after time.' It was inevitable that such fire would soon have an effect and at 1344hrs von Spee's flagship recorded her first confirmed hit on her opposite number. For the British battle cruisers this, the opening phase of the engagement, was a different affair completely as the copious amount of smoke generated by their engines was blown towards the enemy and served only to obscure their targets, giving *Scharnhorst* and *Gneisenau* an unlooked-for level of protection as they raced in to close the range and bring their full batteries to bear.

As Massie notes, Sturdee's intention of fighting outside the capability of the German main armament was a finely tuned affair, with the difference between his 12in. and von Spee's 8.2in. guns being a mere 3,000 yards – a distance that could be traversed at speed – and as the two enemy ships forged ever forward the British advantage, such as it was, diminished markedly until the British admiral ordered a temporary increase in speed which allowed him once again to open the range to 16,000 yards.

Contrary to all expectations, once battle had been joined, it had been first blood to the Kaiserliche Marine, whose crews showed their professionalism with their accurate gunnery. In response, with the combined expenditure of over 200 rounds of 12in. ammunition, *Inflexible* could boast three definite hits on *Gneisenau*, whilst *Invincible* was able to claim only a probable hit on the enemy flagship. It seemed as if the woeful performance of his ships during the live-fire exercise was coming back to haunt Sturdee, as near misses didn't count in actual combat, and it was clear that at this rate of ammunition expenditure his ships would have little likelihood of sinking the enemy before darkness fell which would give von Spee the opportunity to escape, bloodied but intact.

With *Invincible*'s gunners blinded by the smoke from their own ship, and with *Inflexible* suffering twice over from this handicap, Sturdee now ordered the ships to reduce speed in order to give the smoke a chance to disperse and thereby allow both Danneuther and Verner, who were stationed in the foretops, the chance to somehow co-ordinate their respective ships' fire. For a quarter of an hour or so, the pace of battle slackened as both admirals jockeyed for the tactical advantage which had, up until that point, remained firmly with the ships of the Ostasiengeschwader as they continually tried to make up distance on the lee side of the two battle cruisers. Then the firing recommenced.

Aboard *Kent*, one observer wryly noted: 'I have never seen heavy guns fired with such rapidity and such control. Flash after flash travelled down their sides from bow to stern, all their 5.9in. and 8.2in. guns reverberating after every salvo.'

And yet the situation was deceptive as, despite the undoubted accuracy of the German gunners and the damage that they were inflicting on the enemy warships, the British 12in. shells – each weighing 850lb – would still cause severe damage to von Spee's lighter vessels, even if the shells themselves failed to explode.

With both *Invincible* and *Inflexible* still shrouded in smoke, and trusting that this would serve to cloak his movements for a few crucial moments, von Spee now made a sharp turn to the south, apparently seeking a break in the weather to provide some cover. The ruse seemed to work, with the range between the two squadrons being extended to almost 17,000 yards before the British commander was fully aware of what was happening. Once von Spee's intention became clear, Sturdee ordered *Invincible*'s throttles to be fully opened and for the ship to come up to her maximum speed, signalling that *Inflexible*, the only other ship needing to keep formation with the flagship, should increase speed accordingly.

For another 40 minutes the two squadrons chased each other across the calm seas and, with the range reduced to about 15,000 yards, Sturdee ordered his ships to swing about and fire their port broadsides at the enemy. It was now clear to von Spee that his ships could never match the battle cruisers for speed which meant that running before the enemy in the hope of finding protection in the early evening twilight was disappearing as a tactical possibility; continuing to do so would only increase the chances of either *Scharnhorst* or *Gneisenau* succumbing to a lucky shot from the enemy, leading to a reduction in speed or combat effectiveness and the eventual overhauling and destruction by the larger British warships.

Gamely, at a little after 1500hrs, the German admiral once more turned his ships in order to accept combat on the enemy's terms and, as the guns thundered out across the water, his ships' propellers tore furiously at the water, driving the armoured cruisers steadily onward in an effort once more to close the range to a distance at which his secondary 5.9in. batteries would be able to participate in the battle.

Slowly but surely the distance between the squadrons closed until von Spee had his wish and at 10,000 yards his lighter guns began to fire at maximum elevation, with both of the German ships seemingly concentrating on the British flagship. For the next quarter of an hour *Invincible* was steadily rocked by the impact of enemy shells, one of which sheared one of her forward 4.1in. guns in two, whilst another plunged down through her decks and into the sickbay which, fortuitously, was empty. But all was not going the way of the Germans; with the reduction in the range, and Sturdee's slower speed to allow the smoke to disperse, the British fire became markedly more accurate and the intensity of combat saw both squadrons shrouded in a weird mixture of smoke and water spray which served only to hamper gunners on both sides.

Amidst the carnage, *Scharnhorst* was beginning to suffer badly with ragged holes appearing in her superstructure and one 5.9in. gun being torn off its mount and hurled into the sea, the British fire being so intense that fires started by some shells were being extinguished by water spouts being thrown up by others. Slightly farther back from the enemy, *Gneisenau* suffered critical damage when her starboard engine room took a direct hit and had to be abandoned in the face of tons of incoming sea water.

By 1515hrs it still seemed as if the engagement would be inconclusive which, in itself, would be a victory for von Spee, as the enemy were operating

VON SPEE GIVES BATTLE, THE BATTLE OF THE FALKLAND ISLANDS, *c.*1450HRS, 8 DECEMBER 1914 (pp. 78–79)

Having given the order for his light to attempt to the battle, von Spee had initially begun to pull away to the south-east in order either to outdistance Sturdee's squadron or alternatively to find a break in the weather, under cover of which his two heavy cruisers could escape the battle. After a series of circular manoeuvres, von Spee accepted that he could not outrun the enemy and thus, in almost a repeat of Coronel, the inferior force was obliged to close with a superior foe.

Here, the two German ships, *Scharnhorst* **(1),** flying the Vice Admiral's pennant, **(2)** and *Gneisenau* **(3)** are steering directly for the two British battlecruisers **(4)**, *Invincible* and *Inflexible*, which have pulled ahead of the armoured cruiser, *Carnarvon*, and are advancing in line ahead.

Having closed the range, von Spee's ships have opened up with their main (8.2in.) armament **(5)** whilst pushing forward through largely inaccurate enemy fire **(6)**, caused partially by the smoke generated by the ships themselves. At this distance, the German guns are now beginning to score hits on the British battle cruisers, and shortly both forces will swing into line ahead in order to present their full broadsides.

Unlike Coronel, the outcome of the battle is not a foregone conclusion. At close range, it is a duel between the skill of the German gunners and the sheer weight of the British broadsides, and although both *Scharnhorst* and *Gneisenau* will ultimately be sunk, *Invincible* herself will also take significant damage, with a German shell almost penetrating one of the magazines. The result of the battle, whilst controversial, was a full vindication of Fisher's decision to send two battle cruisers to the South Atlantic, rather than the single vessel, requested by Churchill.

at the extreme limit of their logistical chain. Although he had no way of knowing, many of his ships had been unable to complete their coaling and Sturdee had no real chance of maintaining a lengthy pursuit; at the end of the day's combat – irrespective of the outcome – he would have to return to Stanley to replenish his bunkers. Aware that time was passing, perhaps too quickly, Sturdee attempted to break the impasse by ordering his two ships to make a turn to port and come full circle in an effort finally to dispel the smoke that was so plaguing his gunners. It was a risky manoeuvre that meant that the battle cruisers temporarily presented their sterns to the enemy and, despite a number of fresh, but superficial hits, at 1530hrs the two warships finally emerged from the smoke and, for the first time in the battle, they had a clear, unobstructed view of their antagonists, this time with *Inflexible* in the lead.

Aboard the battle cruiser, Verner noted with satisfaction that, 'I was now in a position to enjoy the control officer's paradise: a clear target, and no alterations of course, no "next aheads", nor smoke to worry one.'

Momentarily fazed by Sturdee's manoeuvre, von Spee countered with yet another turn of his own, this time to starboard to bring his ships broadside on across the enemy's bows, a position from which his undamaged and until now unengaged starboard batteries could join the battle. Again the fire from both sides reached a crescendo of intensity that saw flames blossoming over all of the protagonists' ships and whilst the German gunnery remained excellent and extremely accurate, few of the hits were causing significant damage to the enemy. On the other hand, every 12in. shell seemingly reduced the effectiveness of von Spee's two armoured cruisers, with *Gneisenau*'s maximum speed being drastically cut when she was holed on the waterline and a number of boiler rooms flooded. The resulting list to port meaning that – whatever the outcome of the battle – she would be able to fight only her starboard batteries.

By this stage, *Scharnhorst* had been hit by countless enemy shells and was a ship merely in the sense that she floated upon the surface of the ocean. Obviously taking on water – she was down several feet – her bridge was smashed beyond recognition, with all of her masts and one of her funnels destroyed. In addition a massive hole had been torn into her stern. But with the Imperial Battle Ensign fluttering bravely from a jury-rig, she was still a warship of the Kaiserliche Marine and, despite the damage they had suffered, her guns continued to bark out their challenge to *Invincible* and her consort.

The best view of the stricken flagship came from the two British gunnery officers. On *Invincible*, Dannreuther remarked incredulously that, 'She was being torn apart and was blazing and it seemed impossible that anyone on board could still be alive.' His compatriot, Verner, noted, 'We were most obviously hitting her but I could not stop her from firing.'

In the middle of the shellfire, the halyard holding von Spee's personal pennant was cut and fearing the worst, Märker, on *Gneisenau*, signalled the flagship to ask what the admiral's condition was and was reassured to be told that his friend and commander was alive and uninjured. They conversed for a few moments discussing their position and, in closing, von Spee told his long-time friend 'You were right after all', meaning that he acknowledged that Märker's opposition to the attack on the Falklands had been well judged.

For the next 30 to 40 minutes the battle continued to rage, with *Scharnhorst* taking hit after hit. Even in her death throes von Spee's ship almost achieved the unthinkable when an 8.2in. shell punched into the side armour under *Invincible*'s 'P' turret and, after tearing a 4ft by 2ft hole in the

steel plate, burst into her no. 5 coal bunker before failing to explode against the perilously thin bulkhead separating the storage area from the magazine that served both 'P' and 'Q' turrets. Although it would not become known until after the action, *Invincible* had come within a hair's breadth of being blown in two.

At 1600hrs, *Scharnhorst*'s guns ceased firing and, after a moment's pause, Sturdee hoisted a signal calling on her to strike her colours. There was no reply. Instead, and eerily like *Good Hope* and *Monmouth* at Coronel, the battered wreck that was once the pride of the Imperial Navy began to turn towards her antagonists. With the sea washing over her forecastle and taking on water through several jagged gashes in her once proud lines, the dying ship inched slowly towards the enemy and, as she did so, presumably with von Spee still in command and directing the ship, she sent one final signal to *Gneisenau*: 'If your engines are still intact, flee if you are able.'

It was the last deed of a brave man and a brave ship as *Carnarvon*, finally catching up with Sturdee, now opened fire upon *Scharnhorst* with as many guns as could be brought to bear. In retrospect *Carnarvon*'s intervention

might be considered unnecessary, but the German flagship was a combatant and, despite the punishment that she had absorbed, her colours still flew defiantly from part of her superstructure. At around 1615hrs, the stricken vessel rolled onto her side and then, at 1617hrs, her broken engines still attempting to drive her propellers through the water, she went down taking her crew and commander with her. With *Gneisenau* still firing, Sturdee had no opportunity to search for survivors and at 1630hrs when *Carnarvon* came upon the site of *Scharnhorst*'s final moments she found nothing but a sea covered in debris from the armoured cruiser as she went on her final journey.

For the next 40 minutes *Gneisenau* took everything that the three British warships could throw at her, many of their shells simply churning the water around the battered cruiser, but every now and then one would strike home damaging her even further. It should not be imagined however, that this was a one-sided contest as all of the 8.2in. guns on Märker's ship were still fully operational and by now focusing solely on *Invincible*. The British flagship was taking a number of hits and although many were indeed superficial, there were still a number of marked exceptions one of which – at 1643hrs – buckled *Invincible*'s armour belt and led to significant interior flooding by the bows.

By this stage, the temporary advantage that Sturdee had gained by his last turn to port was being steadily negated by the fresh gun smoke that now shrouded all of his ships and the squadron was effectively firing blind at its sole target. At 1645hrs, and frustrated by his inability to engage the enemy properly, the captain of *Inflexible* pulled her out of the line and, reversing his engines to port once more, found an area of bright sunlight. With a clear view of the enemy, Verner began to direct heavy fire against *Gneisenau* with shell after shell thudding into her shattered hull. The success was short lived, however, when Sturdee signalled that the original battle line should be re-formed.

Aboard *Gneisenau* it was clear to Märker that the battle was approaching its final moments. Even with von Spee's permission, the damage to his starboard engine had meant for some time that he could not flee the field and nor would he, in all honour, having seen his friend, his commander, give his

German shell splinter found on HMS *Invincible* following the battle of the Falkland Islands. (IWM, MAR671)

life not just for Kaiser and fatherland but, on a more human level, in order to give his three light cruisers a chance to escape.

Following the examples previously set by both Cradock and von Spee, Märker now set his ship on a collision course with the enemy flagship and, reducing the number of men manning the engines, served to reinforce his starboard gun crews and the ammunition parties needed to keep them in operation. It was a valiant gesture as by this stage of the battle, the final outcome was no longer in question – it was simply a matter of how this outcome would be reached.

Aboard *Gneisenau*, Busche – the gunnery officer – recorded a hell in which 'the men with their powder-blackened faces and arms went calmly about their duties in a cloud of smoke that grew ever denser as the firing intensified; the rattling of the guns running backwards and order transmitters and the tinkling of the salvo bells.... Unrecognizable corpses were simply cast to one side, the walls splashed with blood and brains.'

By this stage the range had closed to 9,250 yards and at 1649hrs her turrets were running low on ammunition – 'A' (fore) and 'X' (rear) turrets had been reduced to lyddite and armour-piercing rounds respectively – and so Sturdee decided to bring the battle to a conclusion. He ordered *Invincible* and *Inflexible* to engage the stricken cruiser at point-blank range. The firing continued relentlessly as the British battle cruisers manoeuvred ever closer, seeking the elusive 'killing shot' that would end once and for all the enemy's resistance. But still the adversaries traded blows, a British shell tearing away *Gneisenau*'s forward funnel before a German shell slammed into *Invincible*'s bows, further weakening the already-damaged armour plating. And so it continued, strike and counterstrike until about 1715hrs when an ammunition hoist seized up and *Gneisenau*'s remaining 8.2in. guns were temporarily starved of shells. Taking the silence to be a sign of surrender, the British ships also ceased fire but before Sturdee could demand the enemy's surrender, the faulty mechanism was freed and the German guns were once more receiving ammunition. Veering off, the battle cruisers opened fire once again and at 1727hrs a heavy shell destroyed what remained of *Gneisenau*'s bridge, rendering her temporarily out of control.

Unlike Coronel, the Falklands were fought in almost perfect conditions, and here the British flagship, *Invincible*, begins to pick up survivors from *Gneisenau*. (Author's collection)

Wary now, Sturdee's ships continued to close the range as a lone gun, the sole surviving element of *Gneisenau*'s main armament, continued to bark out a challenge to the enemy and, at 1750hrs, having taken further hits from the British ships, the battered vessel stopped dead in the water and the enemy flagship raised the signal to cease fire. It was an unnecessary measure as, under cover of the final enemy broadsides, Märker had given orders for his ship to be scuttled and a number of charges had already been detonated in the surviving engine rooms; the loaded torpedoes had been fired and the tubes left open to the incoming sea.

Slowly, almost ponderously, *Gneisenau* rolled onto her side and – as she did so – the surviving crewmen began to make their way onto the exterior of the shattered hull. Standing amidst the remaining 300 or so of his men, Märker called for three cheers for the Kaiser and then, after a chorus of the national anthem, the order was given to abandon ship.

Aboard *Invincible*, the cheering that had erupted at the demise of the enemy ship was soon stifled as Sturdee gruffly gave the order for silence. Then, as the British squadron approached the cruiser's watery grave, and ships' boats were repaired or lowered, the 'brotherhood of the sea' came to the fore as seamen began to line the rails and side-ropes in order to throw anything to the struggling German sailors to enable them to stay afloat until rescued.

For well over an hour, Sturdee's ships continued in their attempts to pluck the *Gneisenau*'s survivors from the cold Atlantic waters. Of her original complement of over 800 men, only 176 were saved, and neither Märker nor Leutnant Heinrich von Spee, the second member of his family to die that afternoon, were included within their number.

THE 'GENERAL CHASE'

The main part of the battle was not, by any means, over. Indeed whilst Sturdee and von Spee traded blows far out to sea, the lesser vessels also found themselves in a life-or-death struggle. Late in the morning, in a little-known part of the action, *Bristol*, with her engines finally re-installed, and the auxiliary *Macedonia* were sent to investigate three mystery ships that had been spotted some 30 miles to the south of Mount Pleasant. They proved to be von Spee's colliers and whilst two of these – *Baden* and *Santa Isabel* were quickly taken, the third, *Seydlitz* managed to evade pursuit, eventually being interned in Argentina.

At 1320hrs, when von Spee had split his forces, Sturdee had given the order for a 'general chase' and the light cruisers were soon racing across the ocean's surface, attempting to achieve by speed and manoeuvrability what their siblings could achieve only by brute force. On paper, at least, it was indeed a 'stern chase' in the traditional manner as all six ships pushed their engines to the limit and respectively increased or reduced the distance between them. However the German cruisers had had little or no chance to conduct any repairs or maintenance since leaving Tsingtao and they were unable to maintain their design speed which was superior to the entire enemy's with the exception of *Glasgow*. In order to cope with this deficit, stokers on the British warships were not only dousing the coal with oil to coax every ounce of power from the engines, but also cast anything flammable into the furnaces to compensate for the interrupted coaling.

For a little over two hours *Dresden* led the line of ships, being closely followed by *Nürnberg* and *Leipzig* and with *Glasgow* leading the pursuers. Then at around 1545hrs the German light cruisers split from *Dresden* turning south-west whilst her consorts turned, respectively, east and southwards and, as the senior officer, Luce in *Glasgow*, by now over 4 miles ahead of *Cornwall* and *Kent*, was forced to make a command decision.

Held back by the two heavier vessels, there was no way that he could catch all three of the enemy cruisers so he was forced to acknowledge that *Dresden* was possibly too far ahead to be caught. Therefore he decided to concentrate with *Glasgow* and *Cornwall* on chasing *Leipzig*, whilst *Kent* went off in pursuit of *Nürnberg*.

Following the rearmost German cruiser, *Glasgow* and *Cornwall* began working in tandem to bring *Leipzig* to bay, firing continually with their heavier forward guns. This meant that the only way the enemy vessel could adequately respond was to present her broadside to the British ships. Therefore, whenever she slowed to turn and fire, she not only lost headway but also lost a mile or two of her lead, allowing them to present their own broadsides and use their superior armament against the lighter vessel.

As with all ships in the German squadron, *Leipzig*'s gunnery was superlative, but her lighter armament had little or no chance of penetrating the British armour and, with the range steadily decreasing, *Cornwall* switched to lyddite shells which devastated the enemy vessel. As he closed, Ellerton on *Cornwall* signalled, 'Am anxious to save life. Do you surrender?' The only reply that he received was a single 4.1in. shell, the last of *Leipzig*'s ammunition.

By 1900hrs it was almost over. With his ship ablaze from stem to stern, and with his magazines exhausted, Haun ordered *Leipzig*'s torpedo tubes to be cleared and the sea-cocks opened before gathering the remaining 150 crew members amidships, where the fires were less intense.

The armed liner *Macedonia* originally used as a piquet boat whilst Sturdee's squadron recoaled, she later joined *Bristol* in succesfully engaging von Spee's tenders *Baden* and *Santa Isabel*. (IWM, Q000541)

Seeschlacht bei den Falklandinseln (Letzte Überlebende) (Sea battle off the Falkland Islands [the last survivors]). As the *Nürnberg* begins to sink beneath the waves, a seaman climbs onto a spar waving the Imperial Ensign in a gesture of defiance. (Author's collection)

Tragically, the British captains saw the launching of *Leipzig*'s torpedoes as a further attack. They circled the German ship to ascertain the extent of her damage and, with the Imperial Ensign signalling continued defiance, they ordered their gunners to open fire again, the shells smashing into the assembled crewmen, killing almost 100 of them. Some of the German sailors jumped into the sea but soon succumbed to the cold water, whilst the remainder stayed with their captain who, in order to save lives, now ordered two green distress flares to be fired, which Luce – as the senior British officer – took as a signal of surrender. At 2045hrs he gave the order for boats to be lowered to collect the enemy survivors. Seeing this, Haun gave orders for the remaining crew to abandon ship and, having shared out his cigarettes, lit one and then disappeared into the wreckage of the ship's superstructure. Finally, at 2123hrs, as the pitifully few survivors – seven officers and 11 crewmen – were being taken aboard the British ships' boats, *Leipzig* rolled over and sank beneath the waves after a chase of over 80 miles.

To the west it looked as if *Nürnberg* would easily elude the British pursuit. On paper she had an advantage of 2kts in speed over *Kent*, and was almost 10 miles ahead of her pursuer, but she had had little or no chance to overhaul her engines during the previous six months and so, with Captain John Allen exhorting his men to almost Herculean efforts, the ageing British cruiser – with her engines working at well beyond accepted safety levels – slowly but surely gained ground on her more modern foe.

At around 1700hrs with mist forming and rain drizzling down from a rapidly overcast sky, *Nürnberg*'s stern battery opened fire on *Kent*, scoring a number of hits, but even at 12,000 yards, the British cruiser's heavier guns were still out of range and Allen had to push his ship even further to close the distance between them. Shortly after this exchange of fire, just as it seemed

LEFT
The impact of one of *Nürnberg*'s 4.1in. shells, shown here just forward of *Kent*'s forward starboard casemate, penetrated the armour plating but was too light to cause major damage. (IWM, Q045916)

RIGHT
Kent – damage to the officers' heads received during the combat with *Nürnberg*. (IWM, Q045919)

BELOW
The accuracy of the German gunnery is testified to by the damage to *Kent*'s upper decks following the stern chase with *Nürnberg*. (IWM, Q045920)

that von Schönberg's ship might be able to foil the enemy pursuit, the pressure in *Nürnberg*'s boilers dropped slightly and, with her speed dropping to 19kts, *Kent* gained the advantage and henceforth the range began to close rapidly.

Here, as with the main action, there was now only one way in which the German ship could escape and at 1730hrs *Nürnberg* turned to bring her port broadside to bear and began to open up highly accurate fire upon *Kent*, which Allen answered with his heavier guns, firstly using normal shell and then, as the range closed, lyddite, which hammered into the lighter vessel causing the outbreak of a number of large fires.

Eventually the comparative difference between the two warships began to tell and *Nürnberg*'s hull was soon riddled with holes, whilst many of

her own shells had simply glanced off *Kent*'s superior armour plate, causing minimal damage. Despite this, the two ships sailed on a parallel course for almost an hour, pounding at each other first at a range of 2 miles and then 4 as Allen, like Sturdee, pulled away to maximize his advantage. Then, while there still remained hope that von Schönberg might just be able to escape in the darkness, one of *Nürnberg*'s overworked boilers suddenly exploded and, as her speed fell rapidly off, it was immediately clear that there was no longer any hope of escape.

Slowly, as if seeking revenge for her sister ship *Monmouth*, *Kent* slowly cut across *Nürnberg*'s bow, unleashing close-range broadsides of lyddite that tore the length of the German cruiser, creating havoc amongst her upper works. She was soon dead in the water and heeling down at the stern but as *Kent* came in closer to inspect the damage and call upon the stricken ship to surrender, she was hit by a lone German shell, and Allen had no option other than to order his men to open fire once more and at 1857hrs with the ship 'riddled like a watchman's bucket' her ensign was struck.

The cruiser's tragedy was to continue when, as *Kent* approached slowly in order to take off survivors, a number of badly wounded were lowered in her one remaining boat, which promptly capsized when it touched the surface of the water. The British warship herself then launched two of her own boats which had been hurriedly repaired and, as they came into view, von Schönberg called the survivors together and after giving three loud cheers for the Kaiser he gave permission for them to abandon ship whilst he re-entered the wreckage of his bridge to await the end.

Slowly *Nürnberg* began to settle by the bows and, as she did so, one of the German sailors climbed onto a stanchion waving an Imperial Battle Ensign fixed to a spar of wood. At 1927hrs, with the light of her many fires being extinguished by the incoming sea, she turned slowly onto her side and gradually disappeared from view. In deteriorating conditions *Kent*'s boat crews did their best to rescue the survivors from the freezing water until 2100hrs when Allen finally called off the search; only 12 men had been plucked from the icy sea, almost half of whom would later die of their wounds and exposure.

And so ended the battle of the Falkland Islands, the most fitting epitaph being that of Surgeon Thomas Dixon of *Kent* when he described *Nürnberg*'s final hours: 'The Enemy fought splendidly, but were outclassed.'

It is an epitaph that could and should also be applied to Cradock and von Spee and to the captains and crews of *Good Hope* and *Monmouth*, of *Scharnhorst*, *Gneisenau* and *Leipzig*.

Typical of the world's press, the front page of the *New York Sun* puts the British naval victory at centre stage, erasing the hitherto lacklustre performance by the Senior Service. (Author's collection)

AFTERMATH

With the sinking of *Nürnberg*, Sturdee had indeed achieved his victory but, with *Dresden*'s successful escape during the early evening, it was incomplete and far from the 'annihilation' that Fisher had required of him. Believing that the fugitive cruiser had fled westwards, he continued towards Tierra del Fuego with *Invincible*, *Inflexible* and *Bristol* but on 10 December, with the weather worsening and with his ships critically low on coal, he gave orders to abandon the chase and return to the Falklands where it was found that one of *Gneisenau*'s shells had torn a hole, some 6 feet by 7 feet, in *Invincible*'s side, just above the waterline. It was her second lucky escape in as many days as the heavy seas off Tierra del Fuego could easily have compounded the damage and caused the British flagship severe, if not fatal, problems.

Early on 13 December, a message was received from Punta Arenas to the effect that *Dresden* had coaled there the previous day, and immediately *Inflexible*, *Glasgow* and *Bristol* were sent off in pursuit but their target had already flown. Two days later, Sturdee left the scene of his victory, sailing to Gibraltar where *Invincible* went into dry dock, whilst he himself returned to what he perceived would be a hero's welcome.

If anything, the victory at the Falklands had served to polarize the Royal Navy even further. Whilst it was obvious that Sturdee would be lauded by his allies, and whilst many officers, such as Sir David Beatty, simply referred to the battle as a necessary panacea for the disasters that had overtaken it during the early months of the war, the inevitable vitriol was soon flowing from the pen of 'Jacky' Fisher who wrote 'We cannot but be grateful that the *Monmouth* and *Good Hope* have been avenged. But let us be self-restrained, not too exultant until we know the full details! Perhaps their guns never reached us (we had so few casualties)! We know THEIR gunnery was excellent! Their THIRD salvo murdered Cradock! So it may have been like shooting pheasants, without the pheasants shooting back!'

Found swimming away from the wreck of *Dresden*, 'Tirpitz the Pig' was subsequently adopted by the crew of *Glasgow*, and then at the gunnery school in Portsmouth. (IWM, EPH009032)

After the Falklands and the pursuit of the *Dresden*

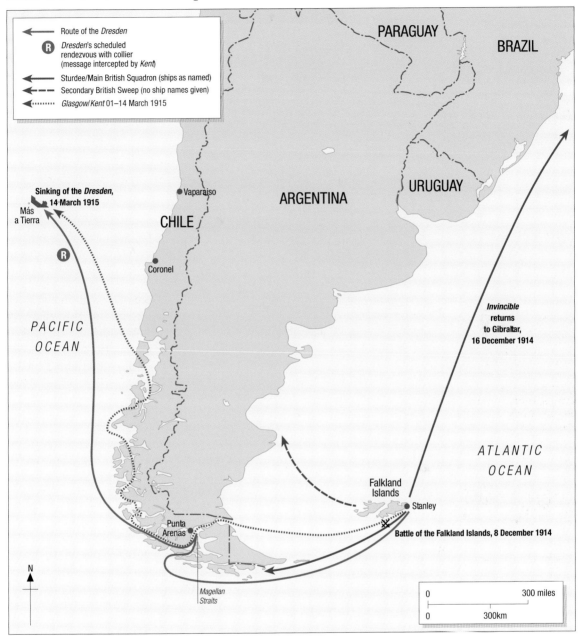

Route of the *Dresden*

Dresden's scheduled rendezvous with collier (message intercepted by *Kent*)

Sturdee/Main British Squadron (ships as named)

Secondary British Sweep (no ship names given)

Glasgow/Kent 01–14 March 1915

PARAGUAY

BRAZIL

URUGUAY

ARGENTINA

CHILE

•Vaparaiso

Sinking of the *Dresden*, 14 March 1915

Más a Tierra

Coronel

PACIFIC OCEAN

Invincible returns to Gibraltar, 16 December 1914

ATLANTIC OCEAN

Falkland Islands

Stanley

Battle of the Falkland Islands, 8 December 1914

Punta Arenas

Magellan Straits

N

0   300 miles

0   300km

The war of words would continue for some time, even after Sturdee received the traditional reward for a naval victory, elevation to the peerage. In 1919 Fisher wrote his final words 'If Sturdee had have been allowed to pack all the shirts he wanted to take, and if Egerton (at Portsmouth) had not have been given that peremptory order, he would be looking for von Spee still!'

After the battle, *Dresden* had fled south towards Tierra del Fuego and, rounding Cape Horn, followed the Cockburn Channel to Punta Arenas where she filled her almost empty coal bunkers before disappearing into the bays and inlets to the south.

With *Invincible* on her way to Gibraltar for critical repairs, Stoddart now took over the hunt and, despite his best efforts, no trace of the fugitive cruiser could be found before *Inflexible* was recalled to home waters. All summer long Luce, Allen and their compatriots edged their ships into lonely bays and inlets vainly searching for any trace of the German warship, and on 8 March 1915, *Dresden*'s luck finally ran out when she sighted *Kent* closing on her position.

A chase ensued but, despite her crew's efforts, *Kent* was unable to keep pace with the fleeing *Dresden*, but even as exultation turned to despair her captain, John Allen, had a stroke of luck. One of his wireless operators

intercepted a message from the enemy ship, instructing a nearby collier to meet her at Más a Tierra in the Juan Fernandez Islands. Radioing Luce in *Glasgow*, Allen made arrangements to rendezvous with his senior officer, and the two British cruisers set course to intercept their prey.

At Más a Tierra, Lüdecke was engaged in a dispute with the local authorities about whether his ship was interned or simply conducting vital repairs, a dispute which became academic at dawn on 14 March when the two British warships hove into view. Noticing that the Imperial Ensign still flew from *Dresden*'s mast, a sure sign that her captain did not view himself to have been interned, Luce immediately gave the order to open fire and an unequal battle ensued which saw the German cruiser heavily damaged before a boat was sent to *Glasgow* under a white flag of truce.

Despite the protestations of Leutnant Wilhelm Canaris who had been sent to remonstrate with the British, Luce was adamant. Unless *Dresden* struck her colours, he would again give the order to open fire. Canaris had no option but to present Lüdecke with the British ultimatum. However, whilst his subordinate was keeping the British occupied, the German captain had made arrangements to scuttle his ship and, as the negotiators returned, the bulk of the ship's crew were busily making their way to shore.

As her crew assembled on the beach *Dresden* sat there, wallowing in the water and then after about 20 minutes she began to roll on to her port side. As she did so, Lüdecke called his men to attention and, after the obligatory three cheers for the Kaiser, the strains of the *Nationalhymne* began to ring out across the bay as the last ship of the Ostasiengeschwader sank beneath the waves and with it the character of the naval war changed irrevocably.

FURTHER READING

Bennett, Geoffrey M., *Coronel and the Falklands*, Pan Books: London, 1967

Corbett, Sir Julian S., *Naval Operations – History of the Great War Based Upon Official Documents*, Vol 1, Naval & Military Press: Uckfield

Dixon, Rose A., *They Fought Them Splendidly*, Blandford: Poole, 1983

Gröner, Erich M., *Die Deutschen Kriegsschiffe, 1815–1945*, Vol 1, Bernard & Gräfe: Munich, 1982

Hoyt, Edwin Palmer, *Kreuzerkrieg*, World Publishing Co: Cleveland, 1968

The Last Cruise of the Emden, MacMillan & Co: New York, 1966

Kirchhoff, Hermann, Vizeadmiral a.D, *Maximilian von Spee – Der Sieger von Coronel (Aus seinen Briefen und nachgelassenen Papieren)*, Marinedank Verlag: Berlin, 1915

Le Fleming, H. M., *Warships of World War I*, (Combined Volume Edition) Ian Allan: London

Massie, Robert K., *Castles of Steel*, Pimlico: London, 2005

Tarrant, V. E., *Battlecruiser Invincible*, Arms & Armour Press: London, 1986

Tuchman, Barbara W., *The Guns of August*, Ballantine Books: New York, 1994

Wyllie, William L., *Sea Fights of the Great War: Naval Incidents during the First Nine Months*, Cassell: London, 1918

Yates, Keith, *Graf Spee's Raiders – Challenge to the Royal Navy, 1914–15*, Leo Cooper: London, 1995

INDEX